MONEY & SURVIVAL.

MONEY & SURVIVAL.

by

"CHAPPIE"

Published by
THIRD MILLENIUM PRESS.
51 Newton Road,
Bath BA2 1RW.

MONEY & SURVIVAL.

Acknowledgements.
To Judith Eversley, Economist,
& my daughter Nina Goodchild

for criticism & advice.

To my wife

British Library Cataloguing in Publication Data.
Chappie
Money & Survival.
1. Money
I. Title
332.4
ISBN..0 9515333 0 4

Printed in Great Britain for
Third Millenium Press by
Anthony Rowe Ltd, Bumpers Farm,
Chippenham, Wiltshire. SN14 6QA. England.

CONTENTS

PART 1

CHAPTER 1
Economic Observations

CHAPTER 2
Transport

CHAPTER 3
Crime

CHAPTER 4
Production

CHAPTER 5
Society

CHAPTER 6
Summary
Valuing ourselves

....

PART 2

CHAPTER 7
Philosophical Observations

CHAPTER 8
Waste

CHAPTER 9
Practicability

EPILOGUE

ABBREVIATIONS

bpk	Billion Passenger Kilometres.
btk	Billion Tonne Kilometres.
bvk	Billion Vehicle Kilometres.
GDP	Gross Domestic Product.
GNP	Gross National Product.
HGV	Heavy Goods Vehicles
PSV	Public Service Vehicles

Unless otherwise stated, 'Man' e.g. Manpower, refers to both sexes.

SOURCES

ASS	Annual Abstract of Statistics.
	Monthly Abstract of Statistics.
DE	Department of Employment Gazette 1988.
	Social Trends.
TS	Transport Statistics, 1976–86; 77–87.
	Passenger Transport in Great Britain, (Now TS).
	Highway Statistics. (Now T.S.)
	National Traffic Survey.
RA	Road Accidents 1986 Casualty Report.
	British Rail Performance Indicators, 1986/7
HIPST	Hospital In-Patient Summary Tables.

Preface

When Sir Thomas More wrote 'UTOPIA' he envisaged a society in which money & property had been abolished, but we, looking backward, can see that had money not been in use, our affluent, technological western world would, in all probability, not be much more advanced than was his mediaeval agricultural society.

Yet his assertion that money is the root of all evil remains unanswered, indeed seems even more apt when we stop to look at the degree to which money controls every aspect of human existence.

Money is a mathematical concept & like mathematics has been of inestimable service in the evolution of mankind, but it is not the real world. We have allowed it to dominate our societies, treating it as omnipotent, allowing it to distort reality & to corrupt our lives. Every few years we are threatened with a stock market crash that could plunge the whole world into recession, yet we cannot tell from day to day what will happen. Just as we have allowed our vaunted technology to take charge of us, making defence against our supposed enemies & against computer fraud so prohibitively expensive as to threaten to nullify both systems, so money itself is rapidly outliving the reasons for its existence.

Because of the way money dominates our lives, the larger proportion of the world population, not only in the poorer nations but some here in the West as well, live in conditions no better - & in some cases far worse - than their forefathers had done two thousand years ago.

Nor is there any sign that we are solving the problem, that things will get better; on the contrary they may get worse. The best financial brains in the world find themselves unable to lift the burden of debt from the poor nations without damaging too severely the profits of the rich. Nor can movements of money be predicted. Our wonderful technology, under the influence of money, has given us so much tittilating trivia that we are sinking in the mess of our own profligacy. Like the sorcerer's apprentice we have become hypnotised, lost in our own bewilderment at the proliferating perils we have unwittingly created. Pollution or the weapons of mass destruction to which we resort whenever we fear that our cherished interests or beliefs are at risk, threaten the continuation of human & animal existence, yet we either hide our heads in the sand or blame communism or capitalism or dictatorship or original sin (other peoples' of course) without considering whether perhaps there is a mote in our own eye or whether there might be basic reasons for some at least of our problems.

Was Sir. Thomas More right after all? Money may not be the root of all evil but there can be no doubt that it is the root cause both of the selfishness & greed that tempt us to claw to our bosoms everything we can acquire, & of the fear, hatred & violence that it provokes against those who might take it from us. At the same time the sight of such wealth provokes in those who have it not, an equivalent reaction of jealousy, envy, covetousness, hatred & violence.

Most of those who read this work, or who hearing of its subject, evade reading it, will dismiss it as Utopian. They will have missed the point. Its purpose is to demonstrate the contrary, that the age of fanciful Utopian day-dreaming is past, that such is our technological capacity for self-destruction that we have arrived at a cross roads, & that money, whether under central control or the free market, does not just create anti-social attitudes, beaurocracy & waste, but is itself inefficient & ultimately totally destructive.

It concedes that even without money to provoke it, the animal in us will affect our behaviour for a long time to come. The age of reason, the day when we are able to control our autonomous animal reactions is a long way off - if ever. People will go on hating each other & doing brutal things to each other because of sexual desires, craving for power, or racist, nationalist or religious bigotry - or just because striking moralistic attitudes gives us a sense of superiority - for a long time to come; but one reason - perhaps the principle reason - for our anti-social attitudes will have gone, giving us a chance to stand back & look at what we were & perhaps to see what one day we might become.

Fanciful? Perhaps! If I were asked to say honestly whether I thought such changes as will be mentioned here would ever reach fruition I would have to accept that in an environment in which we threaten each other with nuclear & biological weapons which we know would eliminate the human race, I would have to answer 'No'.

Would that give me - or anyone else - any excuse however for rejecting the very intelligence with which we find ourselves endowed, that intelligence which gives us the means to conceive, & strive for, such changes?

When my mother was a child & flight was the wonder of the world, Marconi in his yacht off Brownsea Island where she lived was fiddling with the unbelievable belief that he could send a radio message to America. When I was a boy many years before Dan Dare was conceived, the notion that men might walk upon the surface of the moon, so familiar to us, was so ridiculous that, so far as I recall, even my schoolboy comics had few such fanciful notions to stir the fertile juvenile imagination.

The environment is created & changed by human minds, & change itself is accellerating at an exponential rate. As technology changes our environment so our environment changes both our actions & our social attitudes. Given the impetus of even the nucleus of a common will it can change those attitudes in a manner of which at the moment we cannot conceive. Do we have any alternative but to try not just to conceive it but even to create it?

One thing is certain, the choice of whether or not we can retain the social corruption that is money is a luxury no longer open to us. If the human race is to survive it cannot forever cling to concepts which have outworn their usefulness. Adam Smith & Karl Marx lived a long time ago. We have no choice but to find our own way - & soon.

. . . .

INTRODUCTION

Having a common means of exchange has been an essential &, in terms of technological progress, a highly successful human concept. Very early on, gold, & eventually coins, credit notes or bills became recognised as being an easy means of exchanging one scarce resource for another, & quite quickly their accumulation became not just wealth but a source of power.

The need to look for alternative products with which to tempt others has led to technological inventions which have given us the sophisticated western world of today, & it is quite natural that such advances have induced us all to accept monetary systems as being the natural & indeed the only possible means of continuing an ever more satisfying way of life.

Conditioned by heredity & environment, we readily accept the world as it is, for after all we have known no other, & it is difficult to imagine how the world could possibly function without money. For the mind to do so would require great effort & it shies away from - even resents - any questioning of safely established ways & the conception of them to which it has been conditioned. Those ways make its work easier, even if they threaten chemical, biological & nuclear confrontation & total, agonising, annihilation. Usually the day-to-day world we know is more comfortable than any that we can envisage. Even if we live under a dictatorship, usually it is someone else who is affected by any unpleasant goings on. If we keep out of things & attempt no confrontation, we manage to convince ourselves that we can avoid any direct danger.

Then again most people accept that our civilised world, if not perfect, is pretty efficient. To Socialists a perfectly efficient society would be one that was more equal than ours & to Capitalists efficiency, leading to growth, is inhibited by the attitudes of those who do not accept the market economy. But on the whole, whichever way we think, we believe that we are pretty well organised.

Those who live in a Communist world probably believe, even as they wander round their uninteresting understocked shops, that they are fortunate in having more equality than the West. Those who live in the West probably believe, even perhaps as they wander in from skid row to gaze in apathy or envy at the shop windows stocked with all the glamorous trivia denied to them, that they are more fortunate than those poor Commies.

Our world, whichever world it is, is the best of all practicable worlds; yet in a hundred years time or so, when the ball is over, our descendants may wake up, if any of them are left, to find that the glamorous ideal with which their particular ancestors slept, was just a piece of smudged paintwork & will wonder how that twentieth century, with all its potential, could not see what by then will seem obvious, namely that those political solutions, of whatever persuasion, were no lasting solutions to our problems.

Yet it is possible even now to question our accepted views, to create a new systemic model that will allow us to comprehend reality in a new & different way & this work is an attempt to suggest that neither Capitalism, Socialism nor Communism are really as efficient as we imagine, that all the arguments between them are themselves inefficient, a waste of time.

We accept our money world because to us this is the only way in which we can acquire the things we want - or for an unfortunate many, the things we need for survival. But is it the best of all possible worlds? Is it as efficient as we suppose?

Chambers defines efficiency as 'power to produce the result intended', a definition which, for our purpose, itself requires defining. What, in the end, is the result we intend? What can it mean to us, except the maximum long term satisfaction of everyone? That at any rate is the assertion on which this work is based, not on the superficial satisfaction of every trivial desire & the mean-mindedness that too often is its consequence, but the long term well-being of the whole person - & every person, not just the few.

It might be better to use the term 'elimination of waste', waste of what ultimately we look for, which is how we fill the hours which our limited life spans grant us. Such an expression, unfortunately, has become associated in our minds with material waste. Here the wider sense of the word is intended, that ultimately it is our time that is all important & that to waste it on unnecessary & onerous employment or vacuous diversions just to enable us to forget our boredom, is the ultimate waste.

There are two ways in which we can consider efficiency, first from the point of view of the consumer & then from that of the producer. But from both points of view, efficiency does not entirely or necessarily mean the easiest way we can accumulate wealth, but rather how to achieve maximum satisfaction - not just for the individual or even for the greatest number, but for all.

In any system the first consideration should be how efficiency affects the community, for without such consideration, automatic stresses in the body politic are inevitable. The next must be how it affects the individual. Systems, or symbols of them such as money, should, if they are necessary at all, be tailored to both those considerations. Systems should serve man, rather than restrict & enslave him.

It is evident that on this definition money, whatever we may say on its behalf, or whatever it may do for some, does not achieve maximum efficiency. But money has other inefficiencies that are not so obvious. It is frequently argued that human nature being what it is (what is it?), such deficiencies as money has, are the inevitable result of our individual personal deficiencies, & that to think that there is an alternative is to indulge in Utopian dreams. But is it not illogical to create a system to meet our needs & then, when those needs change, to evade the mental effort to adapt or replace it & to blame some supposedly unchanging defect in ourselves? Which is master, the system or the being that creates it?

Part 1 will be an attempt merely to establish the degree of efficiency of our money system. Part 2 is devoted to examining the accepted view that any other system must be impracticable & to trying to show that in a changing world it is inevitable that, over time, the way we exchange one thing for another must change with it.

Whilst care has been taken to back up arguments with relevant statistics, the scope of this work is restricted so that it has been necessary to make certain assumptions. The calculations are not intended to yield actual target figures but to indicate orders of magnitude.

PART 1

CHAPTER 1

Some Economic Observations

Although this is not another book on economics, nor an ethical critique of any particular system, a few words of economic explanation are necessary.

Economics is based on the universally accepted proposition that resources are finite & consist of LAND (soil, climate, mineral deposits etc) LABOUR & CAPITAL (factories, machines etc.) All economic problems arise from efforts to establish the most efficient method of distributing these resources, & money is generally accepted as the medium. There are few aspects of our lives in which money does not play a part, directly or indirectly. Even the water we drink has to be paid for in one way or another.

Two points of view are put forward as to the manner in which money should be regulated to solve the problem of distribution, but neither the market nor central planning have proved to be a complete solution, the first being subject to unpredictable variability, failing to reflect the benefits to & costs for the whole community, & the latter to ponderous inertia.

But some resources are not finite in any reasonable sense of the term, the air we breathe for instance, sea water & its natural products, polar ice & snow, or sunlight. Of these we take what we need or can get without being charged for them. Being superabundant where they are, no one living there could sell them. It follows therefore that the use of money arises from the fact that everything else is scarce.

But is it? For instance, is LABOUR scarce?

13

In 1969 the monthly average number of unemployed in G.B. was 543,800, which was 2.4%2 of the working population, whilst in 1986, even excluding those over 60 years of age, it was 3,161,300 or 11.7%^{DE} of the working population. Between these years unemployment varied around & between these figures, so that we could take an average, over those years, of, say two million as the normal unemployment rate in Great Britain. This is without taking into account those who would have like to have worked but were not recorded as unemployed, young people continuing full time education only because of lack of job vacancies, married short-time workers & those who have been persuaded to take voluntary retirement; but on the other hand there were the registered unemployed who would have had difficulty in holding down a job in a competitive world & those changing jobs. So in G.B. (Great Britain) on average it would seem fair to say that the energies of perhaps two million people annually were not being used.

As we are an industrial nation this means that not only the LABOUR but the LAND & CAPITAL that this labour force might have used, were probably available but were lying idle.

Many reasons for this unemployment are given, government expenditure, trades unions maintaining high wages, monopolies keeping prices high & holding up demand: but whatever reasons are given & whatever the economic theory, they all seem to agree that what was missing was money. For whatever reason money was lacking for investment, whether it was public money or private.

It is a common assumption that money oils the wheels of commerce yet in this case although all the factors of production were available & production should have been at a maximum, it never was. Why was this? Lack of money of course! Yet illogically when there is a surplus of money, prices tend to rise, & this in turn inhibits demand so that in time, full production is inhibited once again. Thus society lives on a sea-saw, trying to achieve a money balance that is continually being upset, sometimes disastrously, by the very checks & balances which are

14

supposed to keep it on an even keel.

Nor can the assumption that money oils the wheels of commerce be sustained in its modern context. To build a barrage across the River Severn would provide enough energy to replace seven coal fired power stations to the benefit of our dangerously polluted environment & provide both a motorway between England & Wales & vast leisure facilities. Such a project is technologically feasible, with LAND, LABOUR & CAPITAL available, but is being dismissed as an unlikely project. Why? Because it would not be financially viable. To give a return on capital the cost of the electricity it would produce would, it is said, be considerably higher than that from existing stations, & in consequence, capital would not be forthcoming either from Government or City. So a project that it seems would provide enormous advantages to life on earth may never be built because of money. Money becomes the decisive factor, not so much oiling the wheels of commerce as clogging them.

Today money has become detached from reality, from the means of creating real wealth, available to complex financial dealings but less & less so to industrial production.

Ultimately it is as customers that we are all concerned. We are of course interested in the manner in which we make a living, but if we were able to live without employment (as distinct from application) we would not be put out too severely. It is necessary here to distinguish between EMPLOYMENT in the economic sense & those activities which we carry out when we are not making a living. Unfortunately & perhaps significantly there seems to be no word in the English language which covers this latter idea. 'Leisure' might imply that we are either doing nothing & so wasting our time, or that we are indulging in some hobby, by implication useless & trivial; & 'usefulness' may not apply either, for that on which we spend so much effort may superficially have no useful purpose. Hence the use above of the word 'application.'

When economists talk about us individuals they lump us all together using the term DEMAND, by which they mean our ability to pay money for some amount of a particular good or service that they believe that we desire.

But economists are specialists using esoteric terms & if we are to avoid being led up some blind alley it is as well sometimes to forget the theories & speak not of DEMAND but of people & their needs, which is not necessarily the same thing.

For instance the term 'ability to pay' in that definition introduces an external factor not related to want or need. A starving African's need for food is not lessened because he has no money to pay for it. The assumption that we can extrapolate automatically from one degree of a given situation to another is fallacious. It may well be that we can justify defending our home from a common burglar, but that does not automatically justify a country using nuclear weapons to defend itself against a nation seeking to take over one of its colonies. Magnitude is a factor which may change a situation. The trouble is that we tend to give such extrapolations a moral character, forgetting that a moral judgement is a value judgement & may look different to different people in different situations. What we shall be investigating eventually, is an economy in which financial, as distinct from resource costs, play no part.

Again economists think of DEMAND in terms of an objective factor regulating production, but demand, like wants, is influenced by other external factors such as advertising or persuasion, appearance or misleading advice, & bears only a limited relationship to need, which I have defined for our purpose as 'a measure of dissatisfaction'.

The only way by which we can examine the efficiency of money is by examining the empirical evidence of its use in each sector of society & how it affects producers & consumers, & then postulating a hypothetical situation in which money no longer controls action. Since in any imaginary situation, assumptions have to be made, & since this is a critique of the money system itself, we have endeavoured, where there has been uncertainty or doubt, to err in its favour.

The first sector we examine is road & rail transport in G.B.

. . . .

CHAPTER 2

Transport

Always in arguments over the relative benefits of road & rail transport it was the financial, not the practical considerations which, in the final analysis, were decisive. Here we take a fresh look at the problem, ignoring finance altogether & concentrating on the resource costs in terms of LAND, LABOUR & CAPITAL.

(1) RAILWAYS

Even if our railways have been a drain on the exchequer for years we can't do without them. We were one of the first countries to have railways. In the peak years 1830-60 a million men were employed in railway construction & 1000 bridges were built, & because railways were a good investment, money was poured into spreading the system to almost every little village in the country, until by 1921 they had reached their peak & had become the principle & dominant means of travel.

Between 1918 & 1939, 23.000 miles of track & 350 passenger stations were renewed, but railways require large amounts of finance & with returns on investment falling, despite concentration into four large companies, which only accentuated their monopolistic powers, they were unable to attract the investment needed for the innovations which would enable them to compete with new, more flexible & cheaper forms of transport such as tramcars, trolley & motor buses, cars & coaches. In 1948 they were nationalised, partly because they could no longer compete, & partly for political reasons.

But then, as with all nationalised industries, a catch 22 situation arose. To keep up to date & able to compete with new means of transport, the money required would have had to have been public money, & to come, in one way or another, from the reluctant taxpayer, so that though there was a clear case for public investment, whether or not the system was needed at the pre-war level, no government which wished to stay in power would provide it. The result was inadequate modernisation & closure of lines, which involved the abandonment of enormous quantities of CAPITAL resources, solely because at that time they were not financially viable.

Logically the railways, with their higher speed potential than road traffic, should have prospered because the population was not only increasing but becoming more wealthy, but they were incapable of competing with a totally different structural & financial system. Rural services declined or disappeared & main line services improved only marginally if at all, despite our vaunted technology. For example, now that the Somerset & Dorset line has been closed, rail travel today on the once direct 65 mile journey from Bath to Bournemouth & Poole, with their marinas & ferries & rapidly increasing potential for tourism & trade, has to be via Southampton, a journey often taking three hours or more.

It is doubtful whether before the war many foresaw the result of the enormous build-up & transfer of traffic to the roads, the millions of cars, the fleets of lorries, the overcrowding, the huge programme of road construction & repair, the effect on pavements & sewers as heavy vehicles try to negotiate & deliver in towns & villages, all, ironically, at the expense of that same taxpayer; yet even if successive governments had had such foresight, it is unlikely that, whatever their colour, they would have had the courage to commit electoral suicide by planning farther ahead than their immediate survival. As for the reluctant taxpayer, he considers that long term-problems are for governments to worry about.

Yet for many years all the factors of production were available for modernisation. With an average of a million or so unemployed, labour, skilled & unskilled was

18

available, just as, in an industrial country such as ours, were CAPITAL goods & resources. Of course without the money incentive the labour force available would not have been prepared to do the job, whatever it was, so that money, or in this case the lack of money, was inhibiting an otherwise perfectly feasible modernisation of the railway system.

Yet there are many hidden advantages, efficiencies in our definition, of a railway system. It is relatively free of noise & chemical pollution & once built is durable & has a low accident rate. It poses few health hazards either for the individual traveller or the public. In general trains can carry large numbers of passengers & large volumes of freight at high speed.

Of course our railways have their inefficiencies also. They are relatively inflexible both in manipulation of rolling stock & in catering for variable loads, & like all large & centralised systems, public or private, British Rail is subject to that curse of any large system, bureaucratisation. The stations are either far apart, necessitating a journey by road to reach them or if not, the trains have to make frequent & time-consuming stops - as anyone who has travelled from Cardiff to Brighton will confirm.

To have combined speed & convenience would have involved laying more track & building more stations, with all that that would have meant in terms of planning enquiries, objections from & inconvenience for the householder whose property would have had to be cleared out of the way, though less, probably than was required for road & motorway construction. In London an attempt to solve the problem by underground railway was only partially successful even for Londoners. To reach central mainline stations, often they have to travel in a direction diametrically opposed to that in which they wish to travel, & then, such has become the size of the infrastructure, have to walk, sometimes hundreds of yards with all their luggage (for porters have become uneconomic!) before they can start any long journeys. The rest of us coming in from the provinces on main lines, similarly have to change stations, with all the inconvenience that that entails.

The restrictive nature of the tracks, only one train being

able to operate on one line at any one time, limits frequency of service, & freight transit is slow, but both these & quality of service could have been improved given adequate investment.

So even an expanded modern, efficient railway system might not have solved every problem of road congestion, but at least some of the present advantages which make us opt for road transport would have been modified.

The trouble is that we suffer from an inability to extricate ourselves from the straightjacket imposed by the financial stringencies of the past, & are compelled to add to the existing system in a piecemeal fashion instead of being able to rethink, replan & rebuild in the interest of long term public well-being.

Must we forever be herded like cattle, packed together upon trains & stations? Must we stand, sometimes for whole journeys, or sometimes sit in dirty old carriages that our grandfathers seem to have left on a siding somewhere & forgotten? Must we endure for ever a system in which large numbers of us have to stand crowded together in second class carriages whilst several first class coaches are empty, have to queue to buy a ticket whilst those in front write a screed to their bank managers, so that finally we have to run for or even miss our train? Must we for ever endure tedious coach journeys merely because to go by train can be as much as a hundred per cent dearer?

Perhaps it is not surprising that in 1986 only 7% of passenger distance was by rail or that the freight carried comprised only 9% of the total btk[TS] - for only those members of the public directly involved are greatly concerned, the rest of us being affected relatively little, or only occasionally. Since those who are affected experience these inconveniences frequently they regard them as just part of life. Most of us accept all these inefficiencies, the deaths & mutilations, wasteful fuel consumption, noise, pollution or road & rail congestion, in the same way.

(2) ROADS.

What a strange mixture we humans are. On the one hand we are up in arms in a second over some slight, some situation where we think someone is 'putting it over on us', or over some restriction put upon a liberty that we have taken for granted. Yet on the other hand we allow ourselves to be put to an enormous amount of trouble & expense just because something has been imposed upon us gradually & we have come to accept it as part of our way of life. Either we don't notice it or we just cuss & five minutes afterwards forget about it.

Most of us go to work, thinking it a tragedy if we lose our job, even those of us who hate what we have to do, accepting that it is inevitable if reasonable living standards are to be maintained. We get the car from the garage & drive to work or to the railway station, there to complete the journey by train; or we walk to the bus stop & wait patiently for our increasingly infrequent & unpredictable buses. In 1978/9, 20% of those who went to work travelled between 5 & 10 miles & 2% travelled over 25 miles.[TS] It is likely that some of the latter went most of the way by train & spent their time reading, though even more likely they were working. But for those who travel by car it is a different story, for driving requires total & frustrating attention, achieving nothing.

Whatever means of travel we use, however, we may be sure that nearly all the other workers are making similar journeys at approximately the same time, & that we shall be frustrated by delays, or inconvenienced in some other way. In the days before so many of us had cars we would catch a tram or bus at the bottom of the road & if we had been unlucky enough to miss one, have to wait sometimes for a full five minute for the next. Today, having done away with expensive luxuries like conductors or vandal-proof bus shelters, we have to queue, sometimes in rain or biting wind, because the bus is already late.

Since, usually, we have to pay the driver, the queue builds up as the bus gets later still, until the one following, if we are lucky enough to have less than a half hour service, catches up & bowls along empty behind us. It is not uncommon where I live to find a fifteen minute service (we are unusually lucky) with four buses travelling within a few minutes of each other, leaving a gap of the best part of an hour until the next one arrives, only to find ourselves in a queue of cars proceding at a walking pace. Within this suburb we have a main line railway station that could serve this large urban area with the means to get into town or into Bristol in a few minutes - only it was closed many years ago, presumably once again because it did not pay.

So for those of us lucky enough to be able to sit in our cars as the traffic crawls nose to tail for miles, there is plenty of time to worry about being late for work or whether the chap who is trying to cut in will deprive us of our no-claims bonus, or to allow ourselves to be oppressed by the thought that at the end of the day's work all that trauma we are enduring will have to be repeated.

Nor is being on our congested motorways with thirty ton or heavier juggernauts nose to tail on each side an experience likely to soothe the nerves. We don't have to be so hopelessly inefficient (for all that detracts from full & satisfying lives is inefficiency); it is just that, though we may grumble, most of us accept all this as just one of the things we have to put up with in everyday life - until the moment of crisis when we are about to be overwhelmed.

Since 63%[TS] of all households have use of one or more cars it is evident that most of us have some sort of individual transport even if we ourselves can't drive, yet into whichever sizeable town we drive, we accept, even if we live near it & pay local taxes, that we must pay parking fees. In other words we take money out of one pocket to put it in another. All completely unnecessary.

How many hours a week do we spend travelling to work? Three? Thirty? It all depends on whether we live near our work or we commute, but a very modest average might be seven & a half hours a week, which, for 48 weeks in the year, (allowing for holidays), makes 360 hours per person per annum. Multiply that by 21,079,000, the number of people in work in G.B. 1986 [DE] & we have a total of over 7,588,440,000 million wasted hours, a years work for about 4 million men, in which we could have been doing something we enjoyed doing, or that would be useful either for ourselves or for the community. A fast & frequent bus service unhindered by queues of traffic or uninhibited by the need to wait to collect fares, could

22

carry 30-40 people at a time. Yet, once again, most of us accept all the waste & inconvenience as part of the world that has grown up around us.

Some of us remember having bus conductors to assist the women who now, in the interests of efficiency, are left to struggle on to buses holding the baby in one arm, guiding a toddler with the other & lifting a folded pushchair up onto the luggage rack far above their heads with a third - but we are told that bringing back bus conductors would increase our present economic measure of efficiency, the price, which would be unacceptable.

Which is the crux of the matter! Money, instead of being merely a symbol of resource availability, has become our measure of efficiency, dominating not just our thinking but our very lives.

We have mentioned only journeys to work but most of us have the same days or weeks off. Have you ever tried to return to London after a sunny bank holiday, crawling along the M4 say, for hours, stop start, stop start? Fifty years ago our holidays might have been limited to a week in Weymouth or Scarborough but there were so many people using the railways that trains were frequent & cheap - & there was no fear of having a nervous breakdown from sheer frustration; indeed we might even have returned to work refreshed!!

But there are even more obvious inefficiencies in our road system. The average speed in crossing London, a vast area is, at peak periods, as low as 16.9 m/h (all roads) & can be as low as 14.8 m/h. In central London it can be as low as 10 m/h. TS. Yet in the 1830s a horse drawn coach could travel all the way from Liverpool to Preston at an average speed of 11 m/h. (Roads & their Traffic, 1750-1850,(John Copeland)). Not that lack of speed is necessarily the only measure of inefficiency as anyone crossing London today will testify; nor even our nervous exhaustion, fear of accident or of being late for an appointment, for there are also the health debilitating fumes, the waste of fuel, the overheating of engines & the wear & tear on roads & vehicles, all in one way or another a drain upon our resources. And what is it all for? In 1986, 1,093,000 people commuted in & out of London. What were they doing? How many were actively productive, or to put it another way, how many were not manipulating money in one form or another?

Nearly all our road travel has become afflicted by such hazards, whether we are visiting friends, going shopping or travelling on behalf of our employer. Scarcely a day goes by without radio announcements of delays on roads, sometimes for hours, due to accident or break-up of their inadequate foundations: and things are getting worse. It is forecast that by the year 2000 the number of vehicle kilometres by cars in G.B. will have increased by between 14 & 30%, & by heavy goods vehicles over 1525 kg by up to 10% & by light vans by betweem 11 & 27%. By the year 2015, cars will have increased by between 26 & 53%, H.G.Vs by up to 16% & light vans by between 25 & 62%[TS].

If the estimates are in any degree accurate, this will involve either a proportionate increase in road building, at enormous cost in money, resources, land & air pollution, with all the problems that that entails, or in many cases that traffic will grind to a halt. At the time of writing, large scale increases in motorway networks & the admission into this little country of even heavier juggernauts, have been promised. So much for our vaunted efficiency! We who claim that we are superior to the animals, treat our own lives as of even less importance. We are indignant when we hear of cattle being jammed together in trucks but we accept it for ourselves.

All very well it will be said, but is all this inefficiency due to the use of money? Why is it a money inefficiency & even if it is, well, we say, we have to have money to make the system work at all, so we will just have to adjust to new situations as they arise, perhaps stagger our working hours rather more - even if that is easier for managing directors than for shop floor workers. But easing traffic flow in that way merely increases the volume of traffic using the system. It is proposed to build new fast railways from the channel to the north, but this is merely to accommodate the anticipated increased traffic that will result from the opening of the tunnel. Entrepreneurs are now tempted to build short-haul rail lines as was done on Tyneside, & this may ease the problem for a time - at least until, perhaps like the trolley buses, they too become uneconomic & we revert to a worse situation than ever. And there is one inefficiency surpassing any of these. In one year alone, in 1986 the number of casualties on the roads was 320,593[RA], yet we accept all the dreadful suffering for those involved & for many times that number of loved ones, with little more than a shrug of the shoulder. To do anything drastic to remedy the matter would disturb our tranquility & cost a lot of money. Yet what an enormous waste of medical manpower & resources these figures represent. Even if accident rates have been declining, & however far out the forecasts of traffic increase, this waste is unlikely to have diminished to any great extent by the year 2015.

Freight.
In 1986 57% of btk (billion tonne kilometres) went by road, carried by 435,000 H.G.Vs (Heavy Goods Vehicles)[TS]. The effect on the environment, extra roads & their repair, structural repairs, speed, volume of goods & volume of traffic, level of noise, chemical pollution & inconvenience, need no emphasis for anyone who has stood in the vicinity of a main road, let alone near a motorway, for any length of time.

Thus, taking into account all the factors we have been considering it can hardly be claimed that the transport system we have in G.B. is efficient. Without more comprehensive & detailed surveys it is impossible to quantify those inefficiencies with any degree of accuracy, but a rough estimate will give us an overall view & allow us to compare road with rail, & private with public transport, to see how they might have developed without financial constraints, taking in turn each of the criteria of efficiency that we have adumbrated, both for the user & for the public.

As already pointed out, on a conservative basis - & so far as possible all our estimates are conservative - journeys to work cost us the equivalent of 4 million unemployed. If only half of this is waste, the equivalent of two million men are forfeiting time & effort that could have been used either for their own satisfaction or that of the community.

AN ALTERNATIVE SCENARIO.

What then might our transport system as a whole have been like had we not been inhibited by those constraints?

Let us suppose that we had not given up the railway mileage we had in 1921, namely 31,120 km, & since then instead of building 2,968 km of motorways, only half (1,484kms) had been motorway, & the equivalent that was spent in LAND LABOUR & CAPITAL on the other 1,484 km. had been spent on new railway lines instead.

Resource costs in LAND, LABOUR & CAPITAL in motorway & railway construction are so variable that it is unlikely to be profitable here to attempt comparisons, but it would not seem unreasonable to assume that the latter is little if at all greater per kilometre of track than the former.

Length of Rail Track under our proposal.

Thus, since most motorways have six lanes, two hard shoulders & a central reservation, we would, with the same resources, have been able to build two & a half times as many railway lines as we did motorways, so that we would have had $2\frac{1}{2}$ times 1,484 km = 3,710 km of double rail track. This means that the total length of railway would have been the original 31,120 plus 3,710 km = 34,830 km as against 16,670 km today [TS], an increase of 18,160 km.

Length of road under our proposal.

The total road length would have been 347,439 plus 1,484k motorway i.e. 348,923 instead of 350,407km at present.[TS]

THE EFFECTS OF OUR ASSUMPTION.

PASSENGERS (FOR DETAILS SEE APPENDIX A)

Railway passengers.

It is of course impossible to estimate what the traffic would have been today on the railway lines that were made redundant, since although they were financially uneconomic at the time, social factors have changed with changing industries, & with greater leisure, holidays, & tourism. For instance whilst many places on these lines had seen a decline in trade, there is today a great demand for access to air & ferry ports, to seasides, to marinas & to holiday resorts.

Many of them are on abandoned railway lines that were through some of the most beautiful stretches of countryside in the world. Since financial decisions are, by their nature, short term, in the long term they tend to be inefficient. In this case, valuable CAPITAL assets in the form of lines that today would cost billions of pounds to restore, were destroyed to save money without thought having been given to what the future might have required. All that can be assumed now is that on these lines, on average, there would have been the same use as there is on average on the present rail networks.

In 1986, a date most convenient for consistency & availability of data, railways carried approx. 2.15 million passengers per route kilometre. Thus with 32,464 km. of track (open to passenger traffic), & assuming inter-city line efficiency, 74.98 billion passenger kilometres, (bpk) could have been carried, i.e. 44.18 bpk. more than in 1986.

Road passengers.

Motorways carried 63.29 billion passengers on 2968 kilometres [TS] of road. Thus there would have been a loss of 1484 km & 31.64 bpk.

Thus on rail & road combined there could have been a nett gain in PASSENGER traffic of 12.54 bpk or 2.48%.

FREIGHT (FOR DETAILS SEE APPENDIX B).

Rail freight.

In 1986 railways carried approx. 0.99 million tonnes/k. Assuming again the same average use, high speed freight on new lines on our 34,830 kilometres of rail, given the same efficiency as inter-city passenger transport, might well have been carrying a total of 36.87 btk.

Road freight.

Motorways carried 4.96 million tonnes/k. There would have been a loss of carriage on 1,484 km of motorway of 7.36 btk leaving us with 96.74 btk.

Thus on rail & road there would have been a nett gain in FREIGHT traffic of 13.01 btk., i.e. 10.79%.

Thus with no additional resource cost we could have increased PASSENGER capacity by 2.48% & FREIGHT capacity by 10.79%.

It is impossible of course to quantify the effects this would have had on the amount of repairs, alterations, extensions or congestion on roads, for though road use would as always have tended to increase if congestion was less, it is unlikely that it would have been sufficient to have cancelled the effect of the improved rail facilities & there can be little doubt that such a saving of road transport would, other things being equal, have increased efficiency & enhanced the quality of our lives considerably.

1. ENERGY CONSUMPTION (APPENDIX C)

The energy needed for long distance freight transport by road is about five times higher than by rail, & passenger cars deliver fewer passenger kilometres per unit of fuel than buses or trains reasonably loaded.

Energy consumption by road in 1986 was 36.94 million therms per 1,000 km as against 25.43 million therms per 1,000 km by rail. Superficially energy saving on roads under our alternative scenario would be 54.82 million therms as against an extra 462 million therms by rail, a nett increase of approximately 407 million therms or 3.04%.

In practice however, real comparisons, even in the absence of financial distinctions, would be difficult to make. Other factors intrude. It does not include energy lost in generating & distributing energy production, nor are we considering like with like. These figures relate to both goods & passengers, & we could not reliably equate them across road & rail. How would the proportion of passengers to freight have been affected on railways & motorways; what is the energy consumption on motorways compared with that for roads as a whole? We cannot know how many people would still have preferred to use a car rather than travel by a faster, surer & less harassing rail transport if costs were not a factor, & further enquiry would be needed to establish how much higher at the margin, fuel consumption would be at higher speeds by road & rail.

At present, marginal increases in road or rail freight might not be sufficient to alter the relativities nor is a marginal increase in the number of car passengers carried likely to affect the average consumption of fuel. An increase in PSV passengers however, should reduce it, since in general public transport does not run to capacity (though there is a tendency on some bus & rail routes to save money by making some passengers stand), but it would be difficult to make any sort of comparison even in the absence of financial costs.

Without detailed study involving different types of road vehicle, of road & rail network, speed & reliability of delivery & length of time specialised goods would be in transit, as well as taking into account different resources used for the generation of the energy consumed, we cannot know whether or which goods could be transferred from one mode to another. All that can be said is that we would not be justified in claiming that energy would have been saved had we built railways instead of roads.

2. ACCIDENTS.(APPENDIX D)

Road accidents in 1986 numbered 669 casualties per bpk, with motorways 76/bpk) as against 14.4/bpk by rail (normally about 10.6/bpk).

Under our alternative, 2,569 motorway injuries a year would have been saved whilst rail casualties would have increased by 636, a nett decrease of 1,933 or 0.78% for all road & rail.

These figures are far from exact & do not reflect the reduction in casualties per bpk arising from the reduction in road traffic that could have been expected if there had been no fares differentials, so that there can be little doubt that this small percentage decrease would have been much larger, leaving us with an additional 16,676 km of route yet with a drastic reduction (approx. 2000) in the number of casualties.

All this without taking into account that whereas railway accidents seem to be well reported, the road casualty figures do not include accidents not known to the police or which only become known 30 or more days after the occurrence. An enquiry at one hospital revealed that 21% of such casualties had not been so reported, & under-reporting of slight injuries is likely to be higher still. [RA notes.]

Furthermore, these figures only relate to human casualties & do not include damage without casualties.

Little publicity - or thought - appears to be given to the real effect of accidents, either on the individual who, if he survives, may have lost years of active life or suffered years of pain or disfigurement, or on near ones who are left alone or uncared for themselves, & who may have to spend years nursing the survivor on a reduced income whilst they try to establish an insurance claim - often until they too become ill.

For the general public there is the wasteful use of manpower required in hospitalisation & home nursing, in firefighting & police services, & in calculating & issuing income support payments.

Of total days spent in hospitals in England in 1985, 14.3% [HIPST] were due to road accidents so if these were reduced not only would there be saving in hospital & doctoring staff, but in hospital building. It is illogical that British Rail is expressly forbidden to take into account social & environmental benefits, such as the notional financial gain from not killing someone in a road accident, to offset higher production costs.

All this without mentioning the additional cost in terms both of manpower & capital, of vehicle repair & replacement, seldom considered it seems, except perhaps by the insurance companies.

3. POLLUTION.

Emissions by road transport in 1985 were 5,852,500[TS] tonnes.(nitrogen oxide, carbon monoxide & hydrocarbons, lead & sulpher) for 297.65 bvk including, on motorways, 838,078 tonnes (14.32%) for 42.35 bvk. This against 61,000 tonnes for 0.361 bvk by rail. Total road & rail, 5,913,500 tonnes.

Superficially a reduction of 1,484 km in motorway

mileage would appear to give a saving of 419,039 tonnes whilst an increase in rail length of 18,160 km would increase emission by 66,452 tonnes, a nett saving of 352,587 tonnes i.e. 5.96%. These figures however, can be very misleading, for they suggest that (a) emission from high speed motorway traffic is the same as for the average road, (b) emissions from new, trunk line trains are the same as the average & (c) there would be no change in motoring habit even though there would be no difference in financial cost to the customer whether he went by road or by rail. Also, once again, we are confronted with the difficulty of estimating marginal cost. A more effective way would have been to compare the reduction of motorway emissions, which are likely to be far higher than average, with emissions from the presumably more energy efficient modern railways, in which case the assumed savings might well have been much higher. The introduction of lead free petrol, though important, is not likely to justify an argument to the contrary.

Chemicals are not the only pollutants however. Noise pollution is a sadly neglected health hazard. Ask those who live or spend their lives in the vicinity of motorways or indeed any busy urban or main road. The present continuous roar of motorway traffic would have been reduced by half, assuming up-to-date train & track laying technology, without any perceptible increase in noise from the increase in rail network.

4. SPEED.

Lacking detailed information on routes & traffic, one can assume that train journeys are, in general, much faster than road, but speeds, including speed of delivery of goods & passengers, depend upon a number of factors. Railways are inhibited by the delays in organising wagons & coaches at goods yards & the limitations of having single lines in each direction, & consequently on the frequency of operation i.e. the distances apart of each train. Road speeds are inhibited by speed limits, congestion, accident hold-ups, terrain & road surfaces.

Motorways have greatly reduced road speed limitations

on certain routes, but road speeds generally appear to have reached or are reaching their peak. The financial, resource & land costs are so high & the propensity for the increase in traffic to overtake the provision of infrastructure is becoming so serious, that it is unlikely that, even with improvements in technology, the new motorways proposed will increase average road speeds. At present it is the railway which has the potential for such improvements. If, under our alternative scenario, we had had today the extra 18,160 km of railway lines, which could easily have been adapted to computerisation & to scientific & technological innovation, such as the new faster aluminium trains & longer stations allowing more coaches, their increased speeds & capacities could so far have exceeded those on motorways as to have increased still further the demand for additional train services & for the restructuring of existing lines.

5. FREQUENCY

So many factors are involved, location, number of tracks or roads available etc., that comparisons of average frequency of journeys would be difficult to establish; nevertheless it seems likely that in general, coach journeys can be more frequent than train journeys even when they are covering the same routes, & individual car or taxi journeys in this respect can be very flexible indeed. Even so, given an increase in train mileage & reversion to public as against private road transport, increased frequency of all these forms could logically have been anticipated. To what extent traffic on main lines could, with modern technology, approach the frequency of underground systems is another question.

6. QUALITY OF SERVICE

One of our standard complaints about trains is that so often they are late, but perhaps it is a compliment to them rather than otherwise that we expect them to run to time. In fact in 1986 90% of all trains arrived within 5 minutes of scheduled time of arrival[TS]. For some reason we never think to question road transport delays or if occasionally we do, they don't appear to warrant journalistic comment; e.g. times by road to & from London cannot, in view of likely traffic congestion, road repairs, accident delays & other hazards, be other than highly speculative. So an increase in train mileage must improve regularity.

Motor coach seats are guaranteed whilst rail travellers accept that often they may have to stand & be herded like cattle. The existence of half empty first-class carriages alongside crowded second class, makes the continued separation of classes an irritating anachronism. On the other hand, where there are sufficient seats, even second class open-plan railway coaches may have tables, & whilst toilet facilities are standard on modern trains, only a small number of motor coaches provide them. Cleanliness depends among other things on how much each service is prepared to pay to recruit & organise the necessary number of staff, & that, in turn is governed by the price mechanism. Car owners decide their own standards but, finance apart, public transport has the facility to set a higher standard than the average car owner, who has limited time at his disposal, & so quality of service should be high - yet frequently is abysmal.

7. CONVENIENCE.

Size & location of rail & coach stations vary from town to town. Some bus stations, being on prime sites, have been sold off & closed, so that information & facilities have become fragmented & that much more difficult to obtain. Goods yards at rail terminals take up large areas but the stations themselves are not necessarily larger than coach stations. Choice of position of public road transport terminals is wider, though of necessity they have to be fairly central. Increase in rail & decrease in road transport might not therefore, affect land use.

Yet that applies only if we ignore all the other aspects of road use, the land taken up by cars left at the roadside day & night, or garage space for public & private use. On average a car needs about a hundred square feet & an average lorry, bus or coach probably 250 square feet so that at any one time our 17 million cars & vans & 435,000 lorries occupy a total of 84 square miles of mostly prime urban land & consequently, for us all, create inconvenience & inefficiency.

The most convenient form of short haul transport for the individual remains the car or taxi, despite road congestion, difficulty in parking in towns, accident liability & limited capacity, &, for the owner, responsibility for maintenance, since these operations provide the only service in which the user can be taken door to door, either direct to his destination or to or from a railway or coach station.

8. VOLUME OF GOODS

Passenger or freight volume per individual journey, is higher by rail, but road transport is more flexible in that the numbers of vehicles, coaches or lorries can be varied easily. Nevertheless it is likely that, with price differentials & restrictions no longer a factor, & given an expanded rail network, railways could have been expected to have recovered some of the trade in goods, whilst passenger increase would seem inevitable.

9. MANPOWER (APPENDIX E)

In 1986 the railway system, for which figures are clearly laid out, had 160,400 employees[TS], including British Rail Engineering & maintenance, but road transport figures are less readily available, & indeed it is impossible to be precise, for with a fragmented & fluctuating industry, the numbers of bus & coach employees & lorry drivers in employment must vary from day to day, & production & support services often depend on vast numbers of volatile private firms. Thus the total number of employees required to maintain road services is likely to be well in excess of the 2,294,000 quoted in Appendix E.

In these circumstances any attempt to estimate the effect of a transfer of resources from 1,484 km. of motorway to railway must, with their very different statistic procedures, be highly speculative & it is accepted that what follows would probably, in the event, be highly inaccurate. Yet on what we do know of present relativities we may be able to get some idea of what the numbers of employees might have been. Thus although in 1986 road transport carried 14.3 times the number of passengers & 6.31 times the freight tonnage of railways, it was at the expense of using 14.33 times the number of employees. All this without taking into account that whilst labour required to maintain railway track is an included item, the effect on road maintenance is not.

Even then, where road manpower might increase in almost direct proportion to freight or passenger kilometres carried, an extra load needing e.g. an extra driver, this will not necessarily apply on the railways.

There is another aspect to this. In the above relativities we have included private passengers & drivers. Official figures assume the driver to be a passenger, but these 434,000 passengers need to be driven. What we are doing in effect is to assume that the driver does nothing. Yet he is as much an unpaid employee of the other occupants, or of himself, as the lorry driver, suffering, whether over long or short hauls, the same strains & frustrations & responsibilities. Where money is concerned too often we assume that a saving in cost by, say, making the customer do the work, selecting & transporting his own goods, is real, whereas all it means is that his efforts are ignored. Why do we never value ourselves or our time?

TRANSPORT SUMMARY

Under our alternative scenario we would have retained our original rail network & built 1,484 km each of rail & motorway, & instead as now, having to face the prospect of our road transport seizing up, have, without sacrifice of resources, land, fuel or manpower, more than doubled our existing rail network, increased passenger carriage by 2.48%, & freight by 10.79%. Furthermore we would have had the potential to increase speed, frequency & quality of service yet further, reduced pollution by 5.96% per annum &, proportionately, the toll taken on road surfaces. Most important of all we would have reduced the number of casualties by about 2,000 a year & increased the quality of our lives by eliminating the frustrations, delays & unproductive labour that today waste the limited years vouchsafed to us.

Illogically, a potentially increasingly efficient railway service was run down just as it was becoming more & more needed, with the consequent diversion to over-congested & unsuitable roads, & damage to their infrastructures & those of the towns & villages through which road transport went. Why? Because money & a limited view of convenience, dictated it. Because money has dictated it we have been left with infrequent & inconvenient public bus services, & transport systems that are becoming less efficient as traffic builds up.

In practice financial efficiencies have imposed upon us physical hardship & social inefficiencies because often it was more convenient & easier to jump into a car than to wait for the infrequent bus, or to wait in a queue to buy a ticket for an even more infrequent & overcrowded train: because the time, inconvenience & cost that has to be devoted to registering, insuring, maintaining & driving individual vehicles are not immediate ones: because a long coach journey is cheaper than going by rail.

Since 1953, 14,450 km of railway route have been closed, to be replaced by a mere 2,968 km of motorway route & 5,450 km of dual carriageway, & it is doubtful whether much of this last can be regarded as other than badly needed repair & updating of existing roads that had become totally unsuited to modern requirements. By 1986 15% of trunk roads other than motorway, 25% of principal roads & 15% of rural roads had a residual life under 5 years[TS] (the M 25 had to be repaired almost as soon as it had opened). All this has been in an attempt to accommodate an increase in demand for mobility of the order of 76% in tonnage movement & 168.9% in passenger movement. No wonder that congestion on the roads is becoming worse.

Motorways & roads in & adjacent to towns are now approaching saturation point, & despite adding more wheels the increasing weight of lorries has meant increased destruction of road surfaces with consequent obstruction of the very mobility that was demanded. As an example, on 26 July 1986 one giant vehicle penetrated a mile & a half into the centre of the congested city of Bath where I live, but was too long to negotiate the turns & had to be escorted as it reversed all the way back again. Railways have their problems but at least are free of this level of congestion.

But we have to be careful. It may be true that we, you & I, constantly bombarded by exhortations to become more & more financially efficient, merely become more & more frustrated by the bureaucratic & legal straightjacket in which our expanding financial world wraps us, but what we call efficiency may, even without the financial distortions, have a very limited application. Our view of how efficiency operates is not always clear, for efficiency is like morality or an object in space, it looks different to different observers in different places. For instance manhour efficiency is not necessarily comprehensive efficiency, efficiency to the customer. Doubling the number of trains & reducing the number of cars may be more efficient nationally but it gives no guarantee that the caravan we ordered will arrive more quickly. Finance is only one inhibitor. Reliability & length of time in transit require ability to organise with a minimum of bureaucracy, & this is a skill not easily acquired.

What has been said here has not been with the intention of belittling road transport, bearing in mind that mobility needs tend to increase to fill the facilities available, nor to be advocate for the rail lobby. Today the car & taxi are the most convenient of all transport modes, liberating us all, including the old, the young, & the disabled, into an era of mobility & travel. Taxis, motor coaches, lorries or buses, all are flexible enough to be brought door to door if necessary. The bicycle requires little maintenance & given better facilities could be the most flexible & useful of all. Nevertheless the financial straightjacket which in the past imposed short-sighted closures of railways & inhibited their expansion, imposed also a disastrous disability on the individual, the public & the environment. For the individual traveller, the most convenient, if not the most efficient form of short distance transport is the taxi since for him or her it involves no responsibility either for maintenance or for driving.

Neither is the intention to criticise past or present decisions. Governments, like individuals, are motivated by character & environment. They are compelled to be pragmatic, to reflect the moods & the circumstances of their time; unfortunately today it is money which sets the parameters.

There is a tendency to fly to the defence of the form of transport, whether road or rail, that happens to suit us, but one wonders whether motor transport as we know it has long to survive. Sheer pressure of numbers may well make it imperative that we find some alternative means, for even if there were a railway revival, its use as replacement of or addition to the motor vehicle would be limited.

All the proposals being suggested for solving the problem, toll roads, road pricing, park & ride schemes, restricting vehicle entry to towns, are inhibiting, often discriminatory & usually no more than palliatives.

Looking ahead - for until now we have assumed contemporary technologies - individual travel by flexible, very fast, single, double or four seater computerised overhead transport hovering on smooth, almost frictionless surfaces & powered by some different technology such as electro-magnetism, would seem to be the answer since, electronically controlled, it could be almost completely accident free & admirably adaptable for either long or short journeys. What would have to be decided upon, supposing such a system were practicable, is whether the environment would be more disfigured by such a system than by more & more roads & railways, & if so whether the saving in casualties would justify our putting up with it. Once again it is the value we choose to put upon our lives.

For the present however, the most efficient service would appear to be an all-embracing & frequent taxi, coach & local bus service linked to an expanded rail network.

. . . .

CHAPTER 3

Crime

Crime is one of our most controversial social problems, for it affects us all, yet there is no consensus of opinion as to what motivates individual criminals or how they may be deterred. Opinions tend to polarise between social deprivation & human depravity, but there can be little doubt that much crime comes from the need to acquire something that is desired, either by stealing it or by obtaining the means to buy it.

Crimes of violence should be society's primary concern. In the affluent west where there are basic social security systems providing a safety net, financial losses should in theory be less traumatic, but money has become to seem so important in dictating either living standards, power or status, that the loss of possessions of monetary value, even if relatively insignificant compared to the loser's income, can take on a disproportionate importance, so that each loss is equated with financial rather than real value. Thefts of valuable paintings or items of jewellery are major crimes even though experts may differ as to whether or not they are originals or copies. Money renders traumatic the loss of that which otherwise could be accepted with tranquillity.

In Great Britain in 1986 those 1.2 million persons found guilty of money crimes, comprised 44% of all crimes, but this excluded additional findings of guilt at the same proceedings (although guilty at a number of separate courts is included more than once). The total number of crimes reported to the police in G.B. in that one year however was nearly four & a half million of which nearly 2.55 million i.e. 55%, resulted in conviction, so that the chances against one of us becoming the victim of some sort of crime, directly or indirectly each year are only about one in ten.

It will be argued that not all non-violent crimes are committed for money, being sometimes for possessions, that the criminal steals in order to acquire & keep the article stolen. But there can be little doubt that this proportion is small. Furthermore it is part of our general hypothesis that the articles stolen would not be in short supply. This argument is enlarged upon later.

There is little doubt that the proportion of money-related crimes to all crimes must be reflected throughout the law enforcement system but we cannot say therefore that the time spent by the police on money related crimes is similarly 44%. The number of hours of police time taken to trace a murderer must be many times that taken to trace a petty thief. On the other hand it is likely that a major fraud investigation would take as long to complete as a murder investigation.

Unfortunately information on which we can make any detailed statement on police time is not available, & I understand that it will be many years before there will be statistics which will give us even a crude estimate. One has no recourse therefore but to assume that of time taken by all sectors of law enforcement in 1986, the police (numbering 135,274), the law, (about 61,870), the probation, (7235) & prison (21,130) services, follow the same pattern, so that 44% of the time spent on law enforcement relates to money-related offences, a figure that would give us about 100,000 persons who were employed solely to deal with such crimes.

It is impossible of course to arrive at a figure for the time wasted by the criminal in planning & executing the offence or in undergoing the interrogation & defence proceedings to which he is subjected, but it is difficult to believe that the total time thus spent by a criminal is less than that spent in bringing him to justice, if indeed he ever is, i.e. that less than 100,000 such persons could not otherwise have been usefully employed, both for his own benefit & for that of the community.

Thus the total wasted manpower is unlikely to be less than 200,000 & is likely to be much more, & this is to ignore the effects of crime upon the victim. As we have suggested, where money is not a factor, crime & the efforts of all those involved in law enforcement would, other things being equal, be reduced by 40%, affecting not only the victims but the social conditions & conditioning of those families in which illegal acquisition is the norm, being passed on from father to son, from mother to daughter or from sibling to sibling. The reduction in crime must affect all those whom we regard as having an anti-social mental disability.

But what will be the effect on everyone else of the elimination of the acquisitive values associated with money? The number of crimes depends on the number of laws, & vice versa, & both depend on the 'moral' values of society at the time. Will we cease to stand, arms across bosom as we agree over the garden fence that everyone else is less righteous than we? Will the number of moralists decline & with it the cries for punishment, for revenge, for rehabilitation even? How many of us have never been guilty of an offence - how many have never taken home an office pencil or a piece of string from the work despatch room to tie up a bundle we wanted to take home, or have never wasted ten minutes of the time for which our employer pays us? How many laws are unenforceable; how many innocent people wrongly convicted?

With less greed will there be less selfishness, less aggression, less hate? Will laws cease to proliferate, & most, in time, become irrelevant?

. . . .

CHAPTER 4.

Production

MANPOWER

Production is understood here to include both creative manufactures & their distribution, whether wholesale or retail,

In considering the efficiency of money in any form of production, whether from the point of view of the producer or the consumer, the three restraints, the scarcity or otherwise of LAND, of LABOUR & of CAPITAL must each be taken into account.

When we considered transport for instance it was assumed that land, in the geographical sense, was & would remain, scarce. What was not accepted, however was that other forms of LAND, or LABOUR or CAPITAL were necessarily so restricted. For instance fuel in the form of coal is likely to be scarce in this country only in the very long term. LABOUR required to extract that coal is, in a society which has unemployment, superficially at least, plentiful. If oil produced in G.B. were suitable for transport use we could have said that it was plentiful even if the means to produce it were not.

Even an approximate figure for the number of employees engaged in activities associated with money matters in the production industries is difficult to obtain. In large firms it would be usual for wages or contracts staff to be treated as a separate entity, but from the point of view of census or employment returns it is not possible to establish to what extent contract work for instance, is concerned with the financial aspects alone, whilst wages & personnel jobs are often interconnected. How many self employed take account of the time they spend doing paper work & even if they do, how much of it, if any, is not concerned with money?

In calculating the nett output of a firm, the raw or semi-processed materials required have to be purchased & this involves estimating quantities, but staff then have to calculate changes in the values of stocks, negotiating prices, notifying competing suppliers, placing firm orders, & negotiating with sub- contractors & transporters. Finally calculations of duties, subsidies, allowances & levies have to be made. Each individual product requires a different proportion of its staff for the manipulation of financial matters, so that in many firms some of these processes are carried out by the same or interconnected sections.

Just how much of a particular industry is a factor cost (LAND, LABOUR & CAPITAL) as apart from financial cost, cannot therefore be estimated.

It may well be that in Mining & Quarrying for instance, the use of staff involved in money matters is a very small proportion of total man or woman hours, yet plant & explosives & transport have to be paid. In the retail trade however, where there are small profits but a rapid turnover, the proportion of money transactions can be very large, not just at the tills but in pricing items, & in buying & accounting: & the more people there are employed, the more staff is needed to calculate wages.

Miscellaneous services, entertainment, accommodation & catering & cleaning & repairing are direct services & for the most part are manpower intensive, but this does not mean that they are mainly financial. Most are not. A hairdressing establishment takes money from customers & pays wages but the greater part of the workers' time is devoted to hairdressing. These firms have their own methods of calculating output in the national accounts but in a moneyless society would any accounting be necessary? Would we really want to know how many people see a particular film or have their hair cut? Money creates its own raison d'etre, its own avocation.

National Defence as a producer is not questioned in this work, but having said that it might be as well to remind ourselves that if we have not achieved international stability long before the human race has become civilised enough to regulate the distribution of environmentally permissibile output to make money unnecessary, we would all have been destroyed anyway & the problem will have disappeared with us.

In national accounts we speak of output in terms of money, e.g. GDP (Gross Domestic Product) or GNP (Gross National Product). Even without money as a measure of output we would of course, have to have records & forecasts of volumes of production & consumption & of the flow of goods within & across national & geographical boundaries, & to equate them. Volume is a symbol just as is money.

Nonetheless where money is an indirect value, volume is direct & thus more accurate & more directly aggregated. It would not of course give a relationship between one resource & another as does money, but that relationship itself is a false one. There is no relationship between chalk & cheese, only a relationship between their scarcities.

That is not to suggest that we would not have to take into account the factors of production, but at the moment we are only considering the efficiency of money, not just the factor incomes, wages, salaries & income from self-employment, profits, & rent, but also money values of goods, taxes & subsidies, insurance, banking, finance & stock appreciation, customs & excise duties. It can hardly be questioned that even at constant prices money is but a loose reflection of volume. There are always other factors influencing & complicating realities, e.g. double counting (adding money value twice at different stages of production), transfer incomes where payments are made without output, (e.g. pensions), or income in kind where e.g. wages or benefits are paid in the form of food or housing.

It is significant that in national accounts, at least in the West, insurance, banking, finance & business services are regarded as industries although they themselves produce nothing. It could be said that professional & scientific services equally are not productive, but this would be fair only for a limited number of such services, in accounting for instance. Schools & Universities may not be directly part of the production process but they are essential preliminaries to that process & cannot be divorced from it, whilst medical services keep labour efficient. Official statistics implicitly accept this in that the numbers employed in these establishments are weighted according to grade.

We have always assumed that financial services equally are part of the process, that indeed industry could not function without them, but this is not the case. Without education & training of men & women no industry could function at all, but even without money there is nothing to stop production once the materials are to hand & these too can be produced & delivered without money if the will to do so is there. We assume that the world we know, its symbols & its motives, is the only one possible, but man can be master of his world as well as its slave.

Despite all these difficulties one can try to make a rough estimate of the amount of manpower in production which firms have to use to deal with all money matters.

The index of gross domestic product of insurance, banking, finance & business services appears to be about 8.2% of the total weighted output of goods & services. In that case an equal proportion at least of man & woman power must on average be reflected in the financial affairs of the industries for which these services operate, whether they be primary, secondary or tertiary. Obviously it is much higher than that in say the distributive trades or public administration but possibly much less in construction or engineering.

What seems pretty certain is that this figure is an under-estimate since inevitably there must be friction in actually operating the financial services provided. Those who operate those services are professional people who can concentrate upon them & what they do is efficient, but that does not necessarily apply to the individual firms who, in their handlng of insurance matters or investment for instance, may have a less than complete knowledge of the intricacies of these subjects.

A loan may be merely a matter of the bank estimating the future prospects of the firm, which may indeed be a delicate matter, but for the firm the decision to apply for funds might take considerable & detailed investigation & computation over a long period. For banks the issuing of money to a firm for payment of wages is a simple matter but the firm itself has to compute piecemeal, taking into account individual national or private insurance liability for each employee.

Thus for all industries & services it would seem that if we accept 8%, as we will do here, as a working assessment of the manpower required in dealing with finance, we may well be making a goss underestimate.

Thus for 1986, employees in employment, excluding those factors entirely financial or dealt with elsewhere, numbered 16,325,000, 8% of which is 1,306,000 AAS. but we must not forget that there will be less need to build prisons, & none at all to build offices for social security payments & other money serving agencies. Logically the proportion of building work should fall in proportion to the fall in employment generally so that the figure must be well over 1,310,000.

NATIONAL PRODUCTION.

Economists seldom get things right for long & governments, who follow the advice of the particular experts who happen to suit their own preconceptions, either react too slowly or, more usually, over-react.

Thus we tend to have a cycle of high & low levels of supply & demand which in turn depend upon the amount of money in the economy. Usually this leads once again to governments over-reacting.

There is a constant juggling of financial incentives in the relationships between different parts of the economy, & in a situation where resources are or are thought to be, always in short supply, this is understandable. But as we have already suggested, not all resources are permanently scarce.

It is usually accepted that the objective must always be to sustain growth. The difficulty lies in estimating the relationship between growth & the various parts of the economy, investment for example, consumption or profits. Indeed so many factors are involved in each of the components of income statistics that its study has become a major industry.

But each sector of production has a life of its own divorced from the other items in the national accounts. The manufacture of caravans can have little if any direct relationship with education even though we all need to be educated. The relationship between items in the accounts called domestic fixed capital formation only apply if, for instance, there is a shortage in the particular skills or materials required in constructing these physical assets. Making them depend upon each other as a whole, i.e. by bringing in the concept of money, is to hold up total investment merely because of a local shortage.

Again, national accounts can only be produced after the event so that management of the economy has to be estimated upon out-of-date figures, sometimes preliminary & misleading or even conflicting, so that government action to correct one undesirable aspect may be over or under-applied too quickly or too late, leading to another; & so many factors are involved, some of them outside national control, that keeping a balance of resource utilisation can seldom be maintained for long.

This is not a critique of the different economic theories, but we should not accept them all without question. For example, it is not always or necessarily true that the customer dictates the price, that if profits are high more firms start up & the price falls. In practice this does not always work out. A situation can arise where if there are a large number of firms or shops there will be a tendency to operate a small mans' monopoly. Many firms require many premises & many staff & overheads, & in an unwritten & often unconscious understanding they make it imperative that prices are kept stable & high. There is too the factor of convenience. A supermarket with adequate parking spaces can so dominate an area that not even an equally large competitor, lacking those facilities, would find it worthwhile to move in, so that once more we have a monopoly.

Again, to quote the example in the theory of labour, it is said that if hunting one deer takes two hours & one beaver four hours, the price of one beaver is equal to two deer. If the time to hunt one deer is one hour then the price is halved. But if, say, it takes no time to hunt a deer (i.e. there is one in every back garden), then the price would be nil. Your economist would say that in that case the item would be valueless but in fact it is not, simply because we all need to eat. Thus where, as is already happening today, the production of grain is so high that the unit labour cost is infinitisimal, then it has infinitisimally small price value. It is true that some CAPITAL & LABOUR are still required, but to have a price value it must be accepted that people will never grow grain or produce artefacts for any other reason than the accumulation of money i.e. means to buy other goods they need. Once however all goods are freely available this would not apply & we would need to consider what, if any, other incentives would motivate activity. There we have the fallacy of composition, that because the theory of labour is true in a situation of shortage of goods, it is necessarily so where there is a surplus.

We even turn our own doctrines upside down. It is fashionable to extol the virtues of productivity, but productivity is understood normally, to mean maximising production whilst limiting manpower, even when labour is plentiful & resources are scarce. Yet according to theory, if labour is plentiful it should be the last factor to affect output. What distorts our view is money.

How could production carry on however, without money? We have considered what would not be needed & their knock-on effects, the savings in building work, fuel for offices, stationery, tools & cleaning materials. The problem will be how to go on producing the things we shall still need.

Here we must bring in the argument which will have been uppermost in the minds of those who have bothered to read this far. Will anyone work?

We have become accustomed to two impulses that drive us on to work. One is the need to maintain a standard of living & the other the assumption that work is in some way a morally good thing even though for most of us it is usually something to be endured, tedious or mucky or worrying or just hateful.

It is natural that we accept the world as we find it & the world in which we have been brought up is one of scarce resources in which if we want something done we must do it ourselves, individually or collectively. That machines can take away all the drudgery is still barely conceivable to us. But gradually & inevitably machines will take over, producing for us so that our problem will not be in persuading people to work but in persuading them not to work - or more appropriately - to accept that they must find for themselves activities that we do not wish machines to do. We still fail to appreciate the changes that electronics is going to make to our lives, regarding them as incidental, doing our arithmetic for us perhaps, or guiding us to the moon. But life is going to be completely different - &, if he survives, so is Man.

RESOURCES.

Increasingly we are approaching the stage when as we learn more & more of the structural qualities of matter we will learn to fabricate or replicate resources, so that we have to look forward to & be prepared for the inevitable day when CAPITAL, LABOUR & even LAND, will be abundant. We are hopelessly ill-prepared for a world in which there is no limit to the amount of goods, useful or trivial, that we can produce, nor in an over-populated world in which artificial intelligence is taking over human roles, a limit to the manpower available to produce it. What is & will increasingly become limited, is the amount of goods with which we can cope, in effect can hoard or dispose of or that the environment will tolerate in terms of the energy we use to make & dispose of them & the pollution that results.

Even today we have difficulty in getting rid of unwanted matter. In our efforts we send useful things to jumble sales for the poor, or to the third world. The balance, the unusable waste, piles up until we have difficulty in finding anywhere to bury it - after all, who wants waste? If it is toxic & we can't push it on to the third world, we try to bury our heads in the sand & the waste in containers, where our descendants, when they find it, will be able to find out what it is composed of, hopefully before it kills them, & then that they will know what to do with it.

Even if incinerators can be built to cope with the waste

& we can put up with the pollution & other environmental problems that that poses, or it becomes financially viable to recycle it, or governments can impose limits on non-degradable plastics, still there will be so much of it that even if we can stop dumping it in the sea - which it pollutes & comes back to pollute the beaches - the problem will remain.

In third world countries the problem does not exist - their problem is to keep their peoples alive - so that one would assume that the waste accumulation is directly caused by higher standards of living in the richer countries: but this once again is to fail to recognise a root cause, the fact no profits can be made from goods that last. In other words that it is money that, by stimulating production & demand, inevitably creates the mountains of waste. If it were financially viable we could produce plastics that could be recycled, cars, washing machines & other durables that would last until they were technically superceded, & newspapers that carried information instead of the advertisements that propagate the philosophy of the acquisition of trivia. Nor would we have need to produce chemicals that have no useful purpose.

There will always be waste of course but it will be limited as it was before the consumer explosion, to the degradable & the recyclable.

Millions in the world die of starvation or disease because forests are cut down, disrupting the entire ecology of a continent or eventually of the world. Why are they cut down? Because they provide profits: because they provide the indigenous population that previously had been self supporting,with short term means to exist even if in the long term it destroys them: because these people must learn to stand on their own feet: because it is said that free food would bring down local prices & make indigenous production unprofitable. Yet there is or could be enough food in the world to make all these measures unnecessary. Why isn't it provided? Because of money! The food is there, the transport is there, the manpower is there. All the factors which make for the means by which the environment can be protected & standards of living raised, are at hand, yet everything is set at naught because an artificial symbolic element has been introduced, a millstone that we all hang round our necks because we think it to be an essential concomitant to securing or maintaining our standard of living, however low that standard may be.

Nor whilst we have money is the problem ever likely to be solved. The rich western nations, sincerely wishing to help, attempt to do so in three ways, by providing aid but attaching strings to it; by loans on which the recipient countries find they cannot pay the interest as international rates fluctuate; or by controlling their export businesses - & taking the profits. At the same time they cut down on production of food because surpluses create food mountains that cannot be disposed of at a profit - or at least without loss.

We never ask what is the original, basic cause of a problem. Why have we a drugs problem? Because drugs are pushed! Why are drugs pushed? Because there is money to be made from their production & distribution. Take away the incentive by, say, issuing it free on the health service, thus eliminating the pushers, & the problem would go away with it. But no, such a simple solution is not to be contemplated.

A surplus of resources, a surplus of manpower! We can curb the one but what of the other? What of the population explosion?

Fortunately our own experience teaches us that even this problem is not beyond solution. Where the only means by which one can provide for ones old age is the begetting of many sons, families inevitably increase, but sons marry & beget families of their own, leaving fewer & fewer resources for everyone. Conversely in the rich countries of the west in which children are a financial liability & for some people tend to detract from pleasures that they have been persuaded to look upon as important, populations tend to stabilise or even decline. Thus a scarcity of resources inevitably means an increase in population whereas a surplus of resources reduces it.

. . . .

CHAPTER 5

Society.

SHOPPING.

In days past the 'little wife', having little choice in the matter, stayed at home to prepare a meal for 'hubby' when he arrived from work. Without washing machines or dishwashers life was hard for her but within the limited technology of the time it was not inefficient. Whether in the towns or in the villages, all the tradesmen called, the butcher, the baker, the coal merchant, the grocer, the greengrocer, some twice a day, first to take her order & then to deliver it, so that her shopping consisted of trudging a few times from kitchen to front door.

Today, if she wishes to keep up with the people next door she has to go to work. Fortunately our modern efficiency has given us supermarkets & all she has to do is get her car from the garage & travel the two or three miles to the supermarket. There, if she is lucky & there is a car park that is not full, & she can avoid a nervous breakdown trying to park between the white lines, she has then only to push the pram that has thoughtfully been provided for her so that she can save (staff) time, through the crowds & around the shelves searching for the things she has been persuaded by the advertisers that she must have. If she's lucky she can do it all in about half an hour & then can go on to the end of the queue at the checkout. All that is needed then is to drive home. Of course if she cannot drive, or he feels that there will be too much for her to lift from the trolley to the car boot, 'hubby' will have to go with her after his days work. That way she is convinced that she can have a greater variety of the same things & can buy them more cheaply than at the local shop, that is if she ignores the cost of petrol, car parking fees, wear & tear on both car & nerves - and her time, an insignificant item of course, because she sets no value on it .

But that is only the start. The supermarket doesn't sell everything that she wants so she has to go on elsewhere, or make another trip into town.

But even then shopping is not easy. For those of us who work, the shops are usually shut when we need them, at lunch times, evenings, week-ends, bank holidays, or half day or Monday closing, always it seems, when we are in the middle of a D.I.Y. job & realise that we need a reel of cotton or a particular nut or bolt, so that we have either to postpone the job until the next Saturday's mad scramble or spend several hours trying to improvise. But the main problem, apart from getting to town & finding a parking space, is the time we have to spend trudging from shop to shop to find the best 'value for money' for goods which have little difference in what they are supposed to do but vast differences in quality & price - or we fear that they might have. Though dozens of almost identical shops will have the things we don't want, we have to make a special order for anything unusual, waiting perhaps days, weeks or even months before it arrives.

What patient dumb creatures we are, waiting to be served or for goods to be packed, & queueing for that which none of us wants, the privilege of paying, hoping that we shall not have to waste as much time again in going back to complain & argue over unsatisfactory goods. All of us, customers & shopkeepers alike know what its like to be defrauded, legally or illegally.

We have become so accustomed to all these petty difficulties that usually we accept them without protest, but they are cumulative, irritating, inefficient &, in a society which is overlain by an infinity of little complications, the stress they cause is more serious probably, than we realise - & the total amount of time & effort wasted is incalculable.

HOUSING & HEALTH.

Such inefficiencies are all-pervading. Money is so inextricably bound up with our lives that it would be almost impossible to obtain an accurate figure for, say, the waste of our time that we spend in manipulating it. We need houses & have the materials & manpower available - in the latter case anxious - to build them but we cannot build because the majority of those who need them cannot afford them. We have all the factors of production needed to provide homes for everyone yet in G.B. in 1986 there were 120,000 homeless households - not counting those living in overcrowded or unsuitable conditions but excluded from the official definition of homelessness - & in London alone the number of individuals sleeping rough has been estimated at 75,000, & that excluded those sleeping in places not accessible to the researchers. When properties are repossessed by the mortgagors it is not because the houses are not needed any longer by the occupants but because they lack the means or the will to continue with the repayments.

We can afford to fly men to the moon, yet in New York alone, in perhaps the richest country in the world there are said to be some 810,000 homeless.

There are estimated to be 80 million people in the world who have insufficient food yet we cut back on food production merely because we cannot get a price for it, sparing them only such minimum charity as our consciences dictate.

In that rich conglomerate, the E.E.C. the number of people living in poverty increased from 38 million to 45 million from 1975-85 (Studies by the Organisation for Economic Co-operation & Development, Guardian 3.6.88).

It is perhaps salutory to remember that in 1986 the number of people in G.B. on the then Supplementary Benefit, regarded as the minimum income for civilised existence, was 8,291,000 which is 15% of the population i.e. one in every 6-7 persons was on the poverty line & that did not include those who were working but had a level of income no higher. Perhaps that alone is sufficient reason why one should refrain from ignoring any enquiry such as this which questions our present assumptions.

We provide the money & the technology to move men around in space yet spare little to give mobility to the blind & disabled. We could have the skilled manpower to monitor the healths of each of us throughout our lives, but despite knowing that health hazards & deaths are higher for manual workers & the unemployed, with their low pay, poor housing & diet & general deprivation, than for non manual workers, rectifying the situation would cost money & upset our economic strategy. How many mental disorders are due to the stresses of working conditions, of financial & moral pressures that urge us to keep up with the Joneses or to compete aggressively in an increasingly competitive world? We stand or fall according to our ability to compete or we opt out when we recognise that competition is destroying us. From mental illness in G.B., working days lost rose from 13.26% of all causes in 1981/2 to 16.04% in 1985/6 & the number of days lost in 1985/6 were 55.7 millions or in one year 152,603 man years work were lost in G.B. [AAS.] We cannot of course say how much illness, mental or physical, is due to financial stress of one sort or another or how strong a connection there is between financial stresses & drug taking neuroses & interpersonal violence. It can be argued that the number of suicides actually decline during wartime when, it would have been thought, stress would have been greatest, but that may well have been because we were temporarily co-operative & mutually supportive rather than competitive - or even because money mattered less. But if only 10% of those lost years were due to stress caused by money problems at home or work it means the equivalent of a years work for 15,260 persons was lost - in effect wasted, a figure which, remember, related only to certified illness & took no account of those persons who were unable to face going to work, but did not or were reluctant to, apply for such certificates.

. . . .

CHAPTER 6

SUMMARY.

Thus the waste of manpower resources, for it is men & women with whom we are primarily concerned, can be summarised approximately for 1986 as follows:-

(Note. Where not already covered or a department is not directly & entirely concerned with money matters it has been assumed that only one tenth of its operations are so concerned).

Unemployment (June)	3.103.500
Stoppages,(1,920,000 days)	8.000
Travelling to work (assuming that half the time we spend could be saved)	2.000.000
Crime	200.000
Production	1.310.000
Civil Service	240.000
Local Government	21.000
Health Service Admin	128.439
Health deficiencies	15.260
Banking, Insurance etc,	2.285.000
Total	9.311.199

or 34.29% of the 1986 working population of 27,157,000.

This means that over one third of the entire working population (which incidentally includes H.M. Forces) is engaged entirely on money matters or in other words is employed solely to enable 23% of the British people to produce the things we want. To put it another way, if one third of the working population stopped work there could, other things being equal, be no loss of production; or alternatively if only a small proportion of such people stopped work, national output could increase.

. . . .

VALUING OURSELVES

In our hypothetical moneyless world we have shown that there would be a minimum of 34% unused man & woman power available. But this is not all, for every financial transaction involves two individuals. At present we ignore the customer or public part in every action, for he or she carries out his or her part in what we euphemistically call his or her leisure time. Every time we need to buy something we have to work out relative costs, comparing one retailer's prices against another's. We believe that we save money in the maxi- or super-markets, or 'pick your own' fruit farms, by ignoring the hidden expenses like petrol & making the customer do unpaid work such as petrol pump attendant or shop assistant, or using up his leisure time & turning his home into a rent-free office. How long does it take the man in the street to fill up an income tax form, to queue outside the bank for cash, to read the fine print on his insurance application or claim form?

Every time a retailer asks for our money we have to look for it & examine it & wait for our change & our receipt. Every time we receive a demand for community charge or tax we have to spend our leisure checking it & then writing out the payment & envelope, buying a stamp & taking it to the pillar box. Not long? Multiply that by the number of payments we make just in one week & the time taken in the service of money must be phenomenal. Even our unemployed, whose time, at least to them, is as valuable as ours, have to sign on & to collect their money at the Post Office. For nearly all civil servants or local government workers or social security clerks or banking or insurance workers, there is a member of the public who is at least equally involved

So shouldn't we take into account time wasted by the customer? Even if we ignore double counting, e.g. between wholesaler & retailer, & the fact that the man in the street is less (sometimes cripplingly less) expert than the trained employee, such additional wasted manhours would certainly increase that minimum of 9,311,199 non-productive workers by at least a half, equivalent to a further 4,700,000, bringing our percentage waste to a phenomenal 14 million or over 50% of the working population. Unbelievable? Think about it! You are likely to find many other instances that are not covered here, making that 50% a gross underestimate.

Today direct debiting & other time-saving devices save us much of this time, provided that we are sufficiently comfortably off & sure of our capacity to manage our affairs to use such schemes, but inevitably the day of reckoning must arrive when we have to check our bank balances & our bills, so that the time we take can never be less than the time taken by the shopkeeper or official concerned on the other side of the transaction. For the unfortunates incapable of such intricate calculations, debt becomes an ever increasing danger.

For every wasted hour that we have mentioned as spent by workers in dealing with money there must be an equivalent time spent on it by the public. In other words half the population at the very least is employed in wasteful, non-productive effort.

. . . .

It has already been shown that 34% of those working are wastefully employed so that other things being equal we could increase our production, our growth rate, by 34%. Of course such an outcome would be unlikely even if it were desirable, for growth alone is not a measure of efficiency, indeed we know it can promote inefficiencies, more pollution, more congestion, more damage to the environment & increased trauma. Growth is desirable only if it increases human satisfaction, not if it creates twice as many problems.

We pride ourselve on how advanced we are with our technology that will soon take us to Mars, but even here we betray our inefficiency. In 1979 it was forecast that by the mid 1980s we in the west would be working a 30 hour week, taking 6 weeks annual holiday & retiring at 50 or 55. Education machines would take over from teachers; legal, accountancy & medical expertese was to be computerised making all these professions largely redundant; books & newspapers would be superceded by monitors; universal electronic mail would enable office workers to work from home.

It hasn't happened! Why? Partly due perhaps to the reluctance of professional people to lose the prestige which their years of study have given them, but equally, & quite understandably, to their realisation that their (often very remunerative) jobs would disappear & they would be thrust down to the bottom of the status pile - in other words it's the money, aint it?

We are rushing into ecological & military disaster at breakneck speed, with our technology & our social systems running out of control & our political & financial systems able to make but feeble & ineffectual resistance. We have to find an alternative.

This has been no more than a tentative enquiry. What is needed is a full scale detailed survey of all sectors of the economy to establish precisely the degree to which money inhibits efficiency throughout our economic & political systems, & when that has been done the manner in which we can begin to eradicate the inefficiencies of money will be clear enough to justify action. That does not however preclude us from speculating, as we do now in Part 2, on what such action might comprise & what ultimately would be its effect.

· · · · · · · · · · · · · · · · · · · ·

PART 2

CHAPTER 7

Philosophical Observations

'That action is best which procures the greatest happiness for the greatest numbers.'

Perhaps Francis Hutcheson was being less than fair to minorities; better perhaps if he had said 'That action is best which is designed to give the maximum satisfaction or happiness to everyone affected.'

I use the word 'designed' because it is evident that where satisfactions conflict, some satisfactions must be restricted; for example it would be impossible to reconcile the conflicting satisfactions of the potential murderer with those of his victim, though any action taken to protect the one need not conflict with the ultimate happiness of the other.

Since Hutcheson's limited objective is, even in our so called civilised communities, still largely unfulfilled, to try to extend it may seem impracticable; but every proposal for the betterment of the human race has been called that at one time or another, usually as an excuse for inaction, so that to condemn it out of hand on those grounds would be premature. Indeed, since human societies, far from organising themselves to achieve a reasonable measure of individual happiness, have acquired the potential - & apparently the will - to destroy each other, any refusal to examine carefully a proposal for its betterment, however Utopian & fanciful that suggestion may seem, must itself be anti-social.

This failure of organisation seems strange when, looking back along the few thousand years which have elapsed since the primitive birth of its present rudimentary civilisation, we see that the human race has been remarkably consistent in its perception of the basic social conditions necessary before its members can be assured of a contented & satisfying life span. Thinkers & prophets have, bye & large, agreed that peace & justice necessary to the happiness of the human race can be achieved only in a society based upon the concepts of liberty & equality - logically so, since without equality, envy & avarice are inevitable, & without liberty man can be exploited & degraded.

Opinions as to how these basic concepts could be achieved & applied however, have differed according to the contemporary circumstance, & most suggestions for obtaining them have been conventional & haphazard. During the last century for example, there has been a universal & almost total absence of new political & social ideas, so that even today most radicals claim no more that to be followers of Adam Smith or Karl Marx, neither of whom can fairly be regarded as contemporary. We in the western world, under the pretence of accepting the fundamental morality of liberty, tend to leave things as they are, believing that with all it's faults, our present profit-making, private enterprise system, diluted perhaps by a limited measure of socialism, is the best we can expect - at least in the foreseeable future. Those on the other side of the iron curtain believe that communism offers a little more equality even if they suspect that its claims are or have been offset by limitations of that equally fundament concept, liberty. We appear to have irreconcilable ideas, the more liberty we have the less equality & vice versa.

One would have supposed that the rapidly changing technological & scientific world which we are creating at an accelerating pace, would have kindled a parallel revolution in political & economic & social ideas. If we accept that those objectives of liberty & equality are fundamental, equally we should have been able to accept the problem as no more than a technical exercise in working out the logical application of the two principles, especially since, as objectives, they would seem to be harmless & inoffensive enough. We seem to know where we want to go but to be quite incapable of finding our way there:

perhaps there is some fundamental flaw, either in our natures or in our thinking - or in both.

Yet surely we have reached a stage of development when we might have been expected to have modified, if not overcome, either disability.

Should we then, leave all proposals for political & social improvement to the scientists, the technicians & the experts, just as in the past we left them to the lord of the manor or the boss or to some extrovert dictator or, even more conveniently - to God? But if these scientists & technicians are capable of producing, as a sort of progress bonus, new & revolutionary social & political concepts, such concepts should by now have begun to show themselves: yet the United States of America, which we are told is years of progress ahead of us, seems to have a society even more grossly unequal than our own, its underprivileged living in appalling conditions & it's people plagued by demonstrations & violence.

Is this the social progress which these expert scientific & technological minds are supposed to bring? Perhaps we have reason to question the assumption that they can create happiness for us in their laboratories & workshops, fearing that instead of building machines to serve us they may be moulding us to the purpose of those machines, or even that by using their own images as biological templates for concentrating the human pedigree, they may in time change us so that we ourselves become machines. May we not, in cultivating those sophisticated gimmick-makers, have inhibited the very aims we seek, leaving us with an aimless automatic world in which even the great god Progress will find himself in a cul-de-sac with neither wit not will to turn & grope his way back into the light? Such a world may become sterilised & comfortable, but how will we be sure that we will not have missed some wider, more satisfying horizon.

We know that men engrossed in scientific detail tend to miss the overall implications of their own discoveries: surely it is over-optimistic to expect them to be able to perceive that wider road that leads to human happiness?

But if our leaders, our politicians, dictators, economists & priests have failed & if we are not to rely upon our scientists, to whom may we turn in our search for a means of achieving liberty & equality: upon whom are we to rely?

It looks very much as though we ourselves must hold the baby: yet if all these clever & knowledgeable people have failed, how can the rest of us hope to succeed? The problem seems vast, confused, beyond the capacity of mere modest mortals to disentangle; & yet - is such modesty really justified? Perhaps it is our assumptions, not the problems, that are confused: perhaps, like the politicians & scientists, we fail merely to see the wood for the trees.

We assume that progress toward our objectives must depend on a sort of extended materialism, but human sensibility may be capable of wider views. If for instance natural laws can be explained in simple terms, might not the laws governing the way individuals & nations can live together amicably & peaceably, equally be simple & obvious; might not the hopeless tangle into which human society has wound itself have been the result of our failure to see that we have been conditioned to - & thus have come to accept - the sort of society that we have inherited; & that the tangle may well be less difficult to unweave than it appears? Indeed if scientific progress depends on our acceptance that scientific hypotheses should be the subject of free discussion & experiment, may not social progress depend on our treating social hypotheses in the same way instead, as we have done in the past, of looking upon them as the impracticable ramblings of eccentrics?

This means that if we are prepared to examine the practical possibilities of any action which is 'designed to give the maximum satisfaction or happiness to everyone affected,' we must also be prepared, if such possibilities exist, to pursue them. If then, technological progress is not to be rendered ineffective by social failure, & if we are to achieve maximum social & individual satisfaction, then our emphases must be changed. We must make a conscious effort to examine every possibility of achieving our aims & do it with the thoroughness & - so far as we can - the objectivity, which we apply to our scientific investigations, making a determined effort to avoid those emotional confusions & distortions which are normal to, & inevitable in, our present way of life.

The society that conditions us is totally controlled by money so that it is difficult for us to imagine a world in which money is not all-embracing. Man has the capacity consciously to project himself into the next stage of his development, to shake off the shackles of his past, even perhaps of his nature.

To do so he must look anew at these human societies which, for all their technological advance, seem to have settled into suicidal grooves from which they cannot escape. Even if, individually, our thinking proves to be inept or unworkable, at least it may stimulate other minds to other & better ideas. If we are to think anew however, we must stop denouncing all new ideas as silly or impracticable merely because they are unfamiliar or untried. Our readinesss to call every new idea, every suggestion for adding to the sum of human happiness 'Utopian' or 'impracticable' or to assert that 'man is born to sin & cannot change' may well be caused by fear of the unknown rather than by a rational appraisal of it. It may be derived from an unconscious dread that it will threaten our individual little dam of privilege that protects us from the common mass of worldly worries, a dam which, opened to some new untested theory, may overwhelm us so that our protective mantle of superiority will be swept away & we shall be lost.

Above all we will have to recognise that if in part - however small - our character deficiencies, & we all have them, are derived from environmental influences, then any proposals to change that environment must be examined fully, fearlessly & so far as consciously we can, without bias. Fixed opinions, by their nature, tend to be cruel & sterile. Only open minds can make a better world.

Do philosophical hypotheses of the nature of human beings get us very far? In many of the ways we treat each other we are less than animals, yet ultimately, like animals, the way we behave lies in individual satisfaction. We do what we want to do, what satisfies us, even if we fool ourselves that we are being altruistic. We need to stand back & see what in the long term, is the best way of living together.

Since we all are products of heredity & environment, our characters being moulded by the extent to which the latter has modified or strengthened the former, it is inevitable that we each acquire fixed attitudes that make us evade or reject alternative points of view or disturbing new ideas. We have been brought up with, or with the lack of, money & have all come to look upon it as an essential & inevitable ingredient of modern life. Yet after all money is no more than a symbol, an artefact, to be used or discarded as we think fit, & if attitudes cannot be divorced from personality it follows that we are justified in permaneantly questioning their validity.

COMPETITION

The demand for equality & liberty is not necessarily confined to the troublesome working classes & a few woolly-minded intellectuals in their comfortably cloistered universities & colleges. It even includes some who, themselves well provided for, should logically have been well satisfied with the status quo; yet even if we accept that material equality is fundamental to an ideally just & peaceful society, free of greed & envy, it will be impossible for us to achieve material equality so long as we retain money as our means of exchange, for even if by a miracle money could be distributed equally it would never remain so for long. Some people would tend to save it & others to spend & lend it, until eventually its distribution would become as unequal as it is today.

So we have the situation where it is impossible to do away with the factors which make for a contentious society whilst we use money or any other means of exchange, yet we cannot see any means by which society could function without it.

Whether or not we accept that money is the root of all evil however, few of us would deny that it is inconsistent with the ideal society. Are we not then unwise in writing off its abolition - or indeed any other desirable objective - as forever unattainable? The world is changing faster & faster & that which was impossible yesterday becomes feasible today, & tomorrow its solution may well seem in retrospect to have been simple & obvious. Wouldn't it be more prudent to acknowledge those factors which inhibit social harmony & to watch for changes in the environment which would render obsolete those factors which appear to make them impracticable?

Let us then examine the need for money in its modern context to see whether it is indeed indispensible to our present society. What are the factors which, it appears, make money so necessary?

In the first place, without money a swift & fluid exchange of goods would be impossible.

This is true in one sense, but the opposite is equally true, for since in itself the transfer of goods is no more than an organisational problem, the use of money to effect it must complicate that transfer & render it less efficient. In other words money also acts as a brake on the economy. A hundred years ago when communications were difficult & the law very little in evidence, it could fairly have been claimed that money - & banks as honest catalysts & custodians of it - was essential if products were to be exchanged from one person or area to another; but in a civilization which pretends to be highly organised we may fairly ask whether the money machine has become a burdensome inheritance. Need we look farther than the persistent problems of credit restriction, balance of payments problems, inflation, & threats of devaluation?

Surely with our advanced technology we should be able to find a way of producing & distributing food & clothing without this rather cumbersome device? For instance let us suppose that the supply of money to farmers was cut off & in consequence they refused to work. Without their expert knowledge it might be difficult to keep the entire population alive but it would not be a situation with which any British government would find itself unable to cope, for we have learned how to solve such technical & administrative problems. To extrapolate; if it were accepted that society would be more efficient - & mankind happier - in a moneyless society, is it likely that we would be unable to find a way of providing all those goods & services which we have come to look upon as necessary to our comfort?

If, quite unexpectedly, money had to be abolished tomorrow, certainly there would be chaos for a time but we would not starve & eventually we could so adapt ourselves to the situation, as we did with rationing during the war, that life would soon become tolerable again. Whether in practice the barbarians which we nurture so carefully within each of us would regain the ascendance & we would start, literally, to cut each other's throats in a struggle for more than our fair share (much after all, as we do now) is another question. I am concerned at the moment only to establish that in fact money is not & never has been a necessity of life, & to-day has become a hindrance to it.

Nevertheless it seems obvious that no-one could be compelled to work unless he needed money & that without that compulsion everyone would sit around waiting for somebody else to produce & distribute the things which we all need.

But what do we mean by 'work'? Most of us understand the term as denoting that employment which society requires us to undertake if we are to share in its goods & services. For most of us therefore work is obligatory if we are to live in reasonable comfort, & in consequence our reactions to it vary between mild irritation at the way it restricts our liberty, & complete loathing. Yet in the days when such work was confined to tilling the soil from daybreak to dusk, man accepted it placidly enough: only when people became servants, first of the lord of the manor, then of the industrial boss, & finally of the modern monolithic bureaucratic undertaking, did the chains of work begin to rub & in consequence to be hated.

In general we do not find work itself distasteful, only the circumstances of that work in its modern environment, for even the possession of independent means seldom makes us idle. Few men are content to become Bertie Woosters or Oblomovs; they prefer to go into politics or to join the Board of a Company or to carve out new empires. Nor, generally, do housewives sit about all day merely because there is no foreman standing over them; most of them are busy, not because they have to be but because they wish to be; indeed as the children leave home or mechanical aids reduce the amount of housework, increasingly they become restless & drift back to offices & factories - & since many of them take up voluntary work it is not only for the extra money. In general we recognise that people who try to evade all occupation are sick either in body or in mind, for there can be no happiness without creativity of some sort, whether it is in producing a work of art or a million nuts & bolts.

Activity is so vital to us that we none of us could remain sane & human without it. Those whom we call workshy are really so only in a relative sense, for few even of these, unless they are mentally disturbed, sit inert all day; most of them have other interests & it is usually the fact that earning a living interferes with those interests that makes the so-called layabout reluctant to go to work. The vast majority of us, however much we enjoy being idle, sometimes need mental or physical activity as well. Of course many people feel that their jobs are unnecessary or unrewarding, or that they are not suited to it, & this is particularly onerous where they can see no escape that does not involve a lowered standard of living. The rich have no such problems; either they can step into their fathers' working spats or they can drop out & wait until they find the occupation that appeals to them.

But too often to those who have to earn a living, work is something infamous, something that turns human attributes & skills into commodities to be bought & sold, something which has been forced upon them for the benefit of their employers or remote, rich shareholders who accept with callous complacency, those practices or restrictions which conflict with their, the workers, needs & desires: something in short which has to be resisted & shirked wherever possible. Too many of them associate work with neurotic insecurity & with higher & higher standards to which they must measure up or face the sack. Small wonder that they are torn between prostituting themselves to the highest bidder & avoiding work wherever possible, both attitudes making for social & personal demoralisation; small wonder that they regard work & employers as necessary evils, that the stigma of compulsion & the conception that work is disagreeable is fundamental to their thinking; small wonder that often they demand shorter hours when they do not know what to do with the leisure they have already.

It would appear then that the assumption that work is undesirable & that people will work only for money is valid only in the context of the money-regulated society itself, that even if we were freed from the compulsion to earn a living, we would want to go on working if only because we need the activity & would be discontented if we did not have it.

This is not to deny that some forms of employment are unpleasant, so much so in some cases that we believe that we would prefer the boredom of idleness rather than to continue working - until we were faced with that boredom & could see ourselves rotting under it.

The belief that people will work only for money is fallacious; indeed grumble though we do, most of us enjoy our work, for there it is that we meet others like ourselves & satisfy our need to become social animals, make friendships. Even supposing therefore that money were necessary to our society, it is evident that our attitude to work would still need to be re-examined, that we should have to try to make it part of a full life, sufficient in itself, rather than an undesirable necessity. Yet can our restrictive, insecure attitudes ever be eliminated so long as the employer is seen as a privileged person owning his men as he owns his shares, or whilst the job is seen as no more than a bondage necessarily endured. Shall we ever be able to change our attitude to work whilst the money it earns & in consequence our standards of living, fluctuate with the changes of fortune that go with it.

In the West work is no longer a necessity of life in the sense that we would allow individuals to starve to death even if they refused to work at all, but it is more than ever a fundamental need in the sense that without its intellectual & physical stimulus we would not remain normal human beings. Apart from the moral stigma attached to its avoidance, work is a need which has extended itself immeasurably within the wider interests of our modern environment. Yet we still think of it as merely earning a living; our attitudes have not adjusted to an environment which has little relevance either to feudal husbandry or to industrial production. Today 'work' needs to be redefined in our thinking to cover an infinite variety of activities, activities no longer confined rigidly within age groups, childhood & learning; manhood & the activities of earning a living; & finally retirement, inaction &, too often in consequence, senility. Work must be - & must be seen to be - not an undesirable & unnecessary deprivation of liberty but the activity of the continuous process of living, whether it is called school, study, employment, or the hobbies of retirement.

To say that work is not in itself undesirable however, is not necessarily to refute the argument that in a moneyless society some people would refuse to go to work. It is reasonable to assume for example that those with uninteresting, unskilled or very unpleasant jobs are likely to 'down tools' at the first opportunity.

This would not apply to all of them however: many people like monotonous jobs, for these keep them occupied without interrupting their private thoughts. But even if they disliked the work, for how long would they be prepared to do nothing, especially if they lacked other interests or had wives behind them sweeping them out of the house with a broom?

Haven't we failed, even today, to appreciate the extent to which jobs which are undesirable because they are monotonous or dull can, because of their nature, be replaced by mechanical & electronic aids? For instance, let us consider one of the least desirable jobs, that of public lavatory attendant. It might be said that no one would wish for this work, but if this is so is there any reason why they should be required to do it? Already we have automatic loos which open & close, clean & dry themselves, making any attendant unnecessary. Primitive & inadequate examples already exist that show the way such problems can be solved.

It is equally reasonable to argue that people would avoid the worrying & responsible jobs also. Would young men & women still be prepared to study for many years unless at the end of it they could expect considerable reward or advantage? If not what would happen to the top jobs, the worrying jobs, those jobs requiring special skills arduously acquired? This again is to assume that people take such jobs only for the money. But is it really for gain or personal advancement that we study so intensively when we are children or teenagers. At that age few of us fully comprehend when our parents tell us that we must study hard to get a good job - at least until we have reached an age when we have achieved or have failed to achieve that which we have been urged to do. We comply but are we in fact doing more than learning to compete, learning to conform? Our parents, with the best of intentions, wish us to strive, to excel, to 'get on': only gradually do we relate such endeavours to money, & this to a degree governed largely by how much store our parents themselves set by that commodity.

Superficially this seems merely to reinforce the argument that in a moneyless society no one would study, for if parental concern with money were removed, what incentive would remain? In fact there would be two such incentives, man's curiosity & his desire for recognition.

Whilst the desire for money as such must be acquired, curiosity must be inherent, for any species which had failed to observe & learn would quickly have become extinct & this applies equally to individual members: but curiosity needs to be stimulated by the process of learning, for the more we learn the more we become aware of what there is further to enquire into. Thus if this inherited potentiality was not stimulated & encouraged it would be because of a failure in educational method rather than because for some reason we had ceased to be greedy for money. In other words in a moneyless society the extent to which we studied would still depend on the ability of our teachers to stimulate our curiosity.

The desire for recognition equally may be inherent, though here again there is no doubt that it is stimulated by environmental factors, by the influence of our parents, our friends, our colleagues & our competitors.

In the main we have learned to equate such recognition with wealth, but there is no reason to believe that we would become indifferent to the opinions of our fellows just because none of us had money. We are influenced by a thousand other factors, by ambition, by vanity, by our social conscience & by our interest in our work both for itself & for its many intricacies & facets, its organisation for instance, its mathematical or scientific logic or even for its intrigue. Indeed it is likely that if our parents urged on us the moral duty of taking on dull unpleasant jobs many of those who now pass their A level examinations would be cleaning public lavatories.

Recognition, the approval or respect of other people, appears also to be the driving force behind competition, for even when we compete for material things - other than the basic necessities of life - we desire them mainly because they give us recognition or status.

Most of the arguments for the retention of money are associated with the ideas either that without it competition would dry up, causing the economy to stagnate, or conversely that competition is instinctive & ineradicable & that in consequence there would always be people trying to get on top & secure the things that were in short supply. A moneyless society therefore would achieve nothing.

In both these arguments however we are thinking in terms of our present money environment & indeed it is difficult not to view all problems in this way. In the latter case for instance, we tend to think of competition as a means of distributing resources that are in short supply, accepting that this must be unequal. A moneyless society however, would be impossible unless resources could be distributed as needed. Such distribution would be no more than a technical & organisational problem, difficult perhaps, but not insuperable.

Competition on the other hand makes for individual reaction. Inevitably, & however equal your society, some people would forge their way to the top of their profession & some would become leaders, so that in this sense we could never retain complete equality for long. But here again are we not confusing competition - or leadership, or ambition - with the struggle for money, which is no more than a symbol of them? Before we condemn the abolition of money on these grounds we need to ask whether or not leadership & ambition are desirable in themselves & if so whether there is any reason why they should not exist even if there were no money. Is it not pertinent to suggest perhaps that money tends to entice to the top of their professions some people who have no real interest in them & whose objective is money alone - & who in consequence may well not be the most suitable to practice them?

Whether or not the competitive urge is inherent, we have been taught that the survival of the fittest & the rightful supremacy of the belligerent are the natural order of things, to see ourselves as beasts of a jungle wherein the strong & cunning consume the meek & fearful, to see competition within a species as an essential driving force & to accept that the assertive shall as of right, reap the satisfactions of society. Therefore, competitive selfishness is rewarded & money, the symbol both of success & of satisfaction, is acquired by looking exclusively after ones own material interests.

Whether indeed this is a law of nature or anything more than a side-effect of the kind of economic society in which we live is questionable. Some creatures, we are now told, live among their own kind in contentment & co-operation rather than in perpetual conflict, so that even competition to mate is more a question of trial of ability than a fight to the death. Whether or not the competitive & aggressive behaviours of the human species are inherent or acquired however, it is surprising that by now we have not discovered how to overcome such a crippling disability & to have learned to live & work together in peace.

Nevertheless competition is a fact in our modern society & as such must be taken into consideration if we are to imagine a world without money. We shall have to ask whether such competition is desirable & if not, whether it could be replaced or modified.

For some people competition may well be essential for achieving a full potential, but this does not apply to everyone & certainly since money is an artificial human concept, it is unlikely that competition for money & its material spoils is essential if society is to thrive; the assumption that it is so must be prompted by the competitive money world itself. What evidence is there that our leaders would become apathetic if they were not spurred on by financial competition or that society would necessarily be less happy even if they did?

Without money, competition would still exist if only because apart from the desire to improve themselves, men & women would still wish to excel or to achieve recognition; the urge might be less virulent & assume less importance without the stimulus of potential individual material advantage & the emphasis is likely to be on excellence rather than on material gain, but it would not disappear.

Some individuals indeed would find in the removal of the distractions of the competitive need to secure a living & to please those who supervise them, a stimulus which would permit them actually to increase their output. We tend to overlook that in our present belligerent society, for every winner there must be losers, not only the defeated belligerents but also those inherently peaceful people who by nature do not think in competitive terms & for whom indeed competition is a fundamental discouragement. Wishing only to reason & to co-operate they achieve their best only in an environment where these are possible.

If competition stimulates the competitive minority, equally it must depress the majority who are not competitive, those who, by losing, progressively lose heart, enthusiasm, energy, efficiency, & interest until at last, losing hope also, too often they just drop out, shutting themselves off from society altogether. Is it not possible that a community geared to include the slower pace of such individuals as these might reach its goals sooner? What, in the past, might not have been the potential of those who, defeated & deprived in a competitive environment, had developed in consequence bitterness, envy, humiliation, frustration & despair?

The question at issue then is not whether competition as such is necessary or desirable, but whether competition specifically for money is necessary or desirable.

Since money brings us material possessions, not only does it become the symbol of those possessions but it gives them a scarcity value they may not otherwise possess. Bread for instance is plentiful but money puts a value upon it as though it were not. Thus competition must tend toward a single-minded regard both for money itself & for individual self-interest & few of us indeed can claim to be immune from its influence. In our society money makes all things desirable, not only those which are conducive to our comfort, not only our houses, cars, cakes or drawing pins but all the miscellaneous oddments that we could do without & never notice the loss.

Most of us acquire all these things the hard way, competitively, & once they are gained we clutch them to our bosoms jealously - even though quite often we have lost interest in them in the first five minutes. Possession can become everything & however worthless these things may be they are ours & as such always hold out for us the hope that some day they may acquire some value: to let someone else have them would be to lose a battle in the struggle for survival. Envy & greed tend to make us cling on to everything, until the mass of useless junk around us threatens to suffocate us. No wonder we seem never to achieve those satisfactions for which we strive perpetually.

Such obsessions tend to make most of us unnecessarily ruthless. Let us be honest about it; few of us would not misrepresent himself or break agreements if he had a lot to gain & little or no chance of being caught. Competition for money has its uses, but let us not forget also that it promotes inequalities, primitive ruthlessness, dishonesty, a single-minded regard for wealth & self-interest, contempt for any law which does not protect that self-interest, & disregard for the rights of others.

In a competitive money situation therefore, inequalities provoke on one side envy & on the other indifference to the views & needs of the underprivileged. The extrovert, the possessor, the belligerent who can demand & get the things he wants, usually lacks either the imagination or the desire to understand the point of view of the meek, the introverted or the dispossessed: easier for him to condemn the poor, the weak & the sick than to analyse the reasons for their poverty, their weakness or their sickness of mind or body: easier to call them layabouts, idlers, malingerers or scroungers than to question whether those rich men & women whom we admire as connoisseurs or aesthetes are any different: easier to look after his own interests than to listen to appeals for him to make small sacrifices for the common good, to prevent pollution for example or legal vandalism.

75

These attitudes make social strife inevitable, & strife is not only counter-productive but creates social instability. Competition for money makes all of us, unconsciously, hypocrites refusing to acknowledge for example that the reason why we are Christians is partly that to be seen at church is good for trade, that we support democracy against dictatorship partly because it safeguards our social advantages & our way of life, that we support law & order partly because they guarantee the security of our economic advantages. Little wonder that our principles so easily succumb to graft, influence or solicitation.

Indeed, hypocrisy is so commonplace that usually it passes unnoticed: & our greatest hypocrisy lies in our refusal to accept that selfishness is fundamental to us all. A few of us may be bad we say, but most of us are decent unselfish chaps. We may concede - reluctantly & with reservations - that our political & economic existence is based upon self-interest, but we temper it with the excuse that self-interest is essential to any progressive civilization.

Certainly in an individualistic society self-interest is fundamental to survival, but in a multitudinous society survival must depend also on the ability of the individual parts to modify that self-interest to conform with the wider needs of the whole. If idealistic societies have tended to founder on the rocks of self-interest this, usually, has been because they have retained a means of exchange which has stimulated individual greed & temptation or because goods have been in short supply & the means for an equitable distribution was too primitive. Other material temptations than money might stimulate greed, but if money were to be eliminated at least the particular temptation to greed that money provokes would disappear.

POWER

Thus competition as a reflection of the desire for recognition may well be necessary, but competition specifically for money tends to concentrate that desire & to carry it to extremes: & unfortunately in this situation it also transforms it into a desire for power. Since in our present society the only way we can get the things which we want, whether it be bread or diamonds, is by using money, it is obvious that to possess money is to possess power.

Most frequently power is vested in those families which have large incomes & normally this power is self-perpetuating.

Power is the capacity to interfere with the freedom of others: it is the ability of an individual to control his environment, including the people around him, & to ensure that it remains favourable to his survival & well-being.

Power derives from fear that our environment may control us & deprive us of our property & freedom: & the more property or freedom we have the more there is to lose & the greater the incentive to control that environment.

Most of us have accepted the necessity for power & that there has to be a continuous process of imbalance as control shifts from one individual to another, for the process has seemed unavoidable. Nor usually do we question it if some people, cabinet ministers, J.P.s, councillors, civil servants or employers, have power over us. But is this situation desirable, & if not is it inevitable: must we always be so controlled? Since power is the ability of an individual to control the people around him it must make those people act otherwise than they would wish & since maximum satisfaction for all cannot be attained in such a situation, power cannot be desirable: indeed we know that carried to extreme it can be the cause of terrible suffering.

What do we mean by power? Often there is a tendency to confuse it with other qualities, for example with the natural superiority of one person over others in the sense that he has qualities, brains or brawn or organising ability for instance, that they do not have.

Too often power is confused with organisation. Power is the ability to interfere in the private lives of other people: organisation is the regulation of society for the purpose of achieving maximum satisfaction. To manage a job so that it runs efficiently is organisation; to make a man work at that job against his will is to use power. It is not necessary for example that bus drivers should be compelled to act against their will in order that a bus company shall provide a good service.

Only if we are free can we avoid that which compels us to act against our will or which gives satisfaction to others at our expense, but too often we interpret such freedom as permission to advance our interest at the expense of others, freedom to create a nuisance for instance or freedom to promote a business even though it may be against the public interest. Too often the demand for freedom is used to hide a desire to deny that freedom to others or to be self-indulgent at their expense.

In this sense too the denial of freedom is sometimes thought of exclusively in terms of government power, forgetting that private interest, in its acquisition of money, equally can be powerful. After all it is a simple matter to complain to our M.P. about a government department but there is no one to whom we can complain about our local store except the store itself, unless of course we care to gamble in the long, tedious & expensive processes of law. It is easier just to grumble & to accept our loss.

Then again it is claimed that we have a free society because we have a free press, that whatever we write can be published. But this is an illusion. It is true that we can write whatever we like - as one can even under a dictatorship - but whether or not a publisher will take it depends on the money market. Will it sell? Whatever its importance, if no publisher believes he can make money out of a book or no newspaper editor believes that it will conform with the prejudices of his readers, & so increase his sales, it has little chance of being published so that those prejudices tend to become accepted as incontrovertible. Censorship is there but we are so used to it that we just don't see it. One day, conceivably, technology will solve the problem both of publication & of distribution, but today it is a denial of freedom.

Dictatorships are most likely to arise when the people are so frustrated & confused by all the complexities of their societies that they become neurotic & indecisive until eventually, losing dignity & purpose & seeing no other way out, they hand over their decision making, & with it their freedom, to anyone who appears to be a protective father-figure. Dictators claim to achieve efficiency by cutting through red-tape & it is true that organisational simplicity is the basis of efficiency. We know from experience however not only that under dictatorships we lose our freedom but that its efficiency is short-lived, for inevitably in our money world dictatorship must drag with it nepotism, place-seeking, influence, preferment, privilege, bribery & corruption & that these are the very source of bureaucracy & so eventually of inefficiency. Communist societies have been prime examples.

Since money is the means by which we provide for ourselves & our families, we have to submit to those who can supply it. Thus to have money is to have power & since competition for money promotes that power it must to that extent be undesirable. This is not to say that if money were eliminated the desire for power would disappear but certainly there would be far fewer opportunities for exercising it; & once we took away the fear of power, that power would tend to waste away.

To many people for whom money has become a symbol of security the idea of a moneyless society is alarming or even frightening. Yet this, precisely, is where money has failed us for none of our societies, even the most affluent, has been able to eliminate poverty. We live in a great & wonderful age; we have conquered the earth, we explore the depths of the sea & outer space, our buildings reach into the skies, we can travel faster than sound: & yet we seem incapable of securing for all our peoples even their basic needs or elementary comforts. We have not solved any of the major social problems that afflicted us a hundred, two hundred, or two thousand years ago. Even in the richest countries large proportions of the populations, mainly those who are without work or who are old, sick or deserted, live in damp & derelict houses, or in bed sitting rooms, sometimes without linen, fuel or adequate food, from which they are barred during the day & have to tramp the streets with their children, restricted to a basic standard of living that is forever struggling behind the needs of modern community life.

Will the competitive money economy ever be capable of solving the simple & apparently straightforward social problems of ensuring that children shall no longer go hungry & neglected, that the disabled & the slow of understanding who are the first to be put out of work & the last to be taken back - & often have the least ability to cope with the problems of household management - shall no longer be condemned to having to manage for life on a minimum income, one on which the most intelligent of us would find long term economic housekeeping a daunting task?

It is fashionable to look back with condescension upon the 'dark ages' but historians are beginning to question whether homelessness was rife then as it is today in the West or starvation the problem it is in many parts of the world. Progress?

We build mansions when for the same money we could house several families who live in squalor. Vast quantities of material & of manpower hours are wasted in making thousands of unnecessary cars, choking our roads & bringing injury & death to thousands of people every year & yet it seldom occurs to us that the cost of perhaps no more than two such cars could provide for a homeless family. Is it any wonder that those who have low incomes become discontented & that society is beset by stresses that threaten to erupt into violence?

Often the price of a roof over ones head is the acceptance of a lifetime of servitude, in debt to usurers, moneylenders who hide under respectable names like 'building societies', 'local authorities' or 'banks'. Backward nations which need outside capital to develop, risk a permanent indebtedness & servitude that does little more than increase the wealth of the rich countries from which they borrow.

Most of us are incapable of divorcing the simple task of distributing fairly the basic necessities of life from the complicated machinery of exchange, & because of this obsession with money the more commitments that are acquired in the bid to keep up with the chap next door the more the problems of the poor devils at the scruffy end of the town are forgotten.

There can never be social equality in a money world for, as I have said before, even if at the wave of a wand we could give everyone equal financial status, at once some would start to accumulate money & others to lose it. Equally there can never be social justice in a society based on money for our standards of conduct & of justice vary according to our individual financial circumstances & desires.

It is natural that those who are secure should resist, consciously or otherwise, any question as to whether that which guarantees their security is needed, any more than they care to consider whether their investments might tend permanently to enrich those who have money already & to keep impoverished those who do not. Such conceptions might involve some unspecified but dreadful sacrifice. Yet we don't have to be hyper-sensitively sympathetic to see how frustrating a flambuoyantly extrovert affluent society must be to a starving African or to those who have to stretch out a basic wage to cover the modern needs of a family; on those who have to walk whilst others drive; on those who have to watch every penny every day of the week, not for just a year, but for a lifetime; on those who have always to queue or go without in times of shortage; or on those who know that none of the many luxuries stacked enticingly in the shops will ever be for them.

Often it is those least able to manage that seem always to have the least money to manage on, the old, the sick, the mentally handicapped, the uneducated, the meek & those who are too weak-willed to be able to say 'no' to tempting shopkeepers, sharp salesmen, H.P. touts & credit companies. Is it so surprising that these people are jealous or disgruntled or anti-social or neurotic, that they are driven to hatred, to meanness, artfulness, theft or violence? Even the meek can hate & be jealous of those who, because they were lucky enough to have been born clever or sharp-witted or have rich parents, for some reason suppose themselves to be superior.

To accept that each one of us is born with individual physical & mental potentialities is no excuse for erecting or accepting additional artificial inequalities. Yet had our existing competitive money society been capable of eliminating these additional inequalities surely it would have had time enough in the last two thousand years to have done so. Can we doubt that if that society still exists fifty years from now, they will be with us still, that the lucky ones who have health, wealth, strength, energy or looks, cleverness or artfulness will still be securing for themselves every opportunity & advantage. If this is the best that the competitive money economy can do, are we really justified in shrugging our shoulders & refusing to seek an alternative?

We set great value on brains & slickness of mind, forgetting that brains are a gift just as brawn or manual skills or meekness are gifts. Is there any ethical reason why those who have them should be more highly rewarded by material advantage than the others? Either we have such gifts or we do not, & if the gift of brains is to be so highly rewarded, why only certain categories of brain? Why exclude the clever scientist working away for a pittance in the lab., or the musician in the local philharmonic? Why are rewards restricted mainly to those who are sharp-witted, cunning, & quick to take advantage of every opportunity for self-advancement? Surely such advantages need no reward - should be taxed even, rather than as now, given tax concessions? Is it reasonable to accept without question that abilities such as these are so indispensable that to discourage them by increasing income tax for instance, or reducing their financial benefits, would bring economic disaster, that they must be encouraged even if they do no more than manipulate money, producing nothing tangible at all, whereas the production worker who strikes for a higher wage is irresponsible & must be discouraged?

Is there any justification at all for rewarding brains more than brawn, pop singers more than opera stars, extroverts more than introverts, or in fact any human being more than any other, for the gifts we have, such as they are, are gifts of God or chance or what you will, more reason for humility than for pride, for making sacrifices for the sake of those less fortunate, than for use as a means of self-elevation? But it is useless to ask for such humility, for we are conditioned to a state of universal & perpetual desire, to accept that aggressive competition is the virtuous means of achieving it.

Why do we accept that those lucky enough to have been born clever or sharp-witted are superior beings? On what grounds can we claim credit for gifts that by good fortune we have inherited, brains or brawn or guts or drive or a pretty face or money or country houses? Fortunately again for them, those who have inherited brains or cleverness or artfulness have the ability to construct arguments to support the status quo - & have money & power to back it up, so that they are able to cushion themselves in yet another impregnable Catch 22 situation.

The snob value of brains has turned the world into an hierarchical structure wherein those with cleverness & those with the good fortune to have been taught how to use the power of imagination so as to enjoy the wider pleasures of the mind, also claim a prior right to all worldly pleasures. Though each book read is in itself an experience that only the literate can know, though learning is a delight reserved for those with the ability to learn, though music is a pleasure reserved for those who have learned to listen, the fortunate people who can do these things have not been content, have demanded the first choice even of the lesser, the material, pleasures. The backward, the sick, the weak & the inadequately educated are denied even the worldly compensations. All the universe is at the service of the fit, the capable, the educated, the cunning: even the mundane worldly pleasures are denied to the disabled, the illiterate, the undeveloped, those who, if they tried to seize such pleasures would in turn be seized upon by the law & even such basic freedom as they have would be taken from them.

If we have brains we have acquired them only by chance. All our attributes, even our weaknesses, are dependent upon our other qualities: we are composed not only of body & brain, but of hopes & fears & loves. By what right have we made Man's cleverness & the pleasures that that cleverness brings, more important than Man himself? Perhaps if we tried to eliminate such artificial inequalities & with them the dissatisfactions & distrust that they create, we might thereby eliminate also the greed & envy of which each one of us has his share.

No individual is superior to any other, & no one is inferior, for all that we have of energy, vitality, beauty or brains are but chance gifts for which none of us can claim credit. Shouldn't we rather be humbly grateful for them, seeking actively to use them for the benefit of the whole community - & not only for now or next year, but for twenty or fifty or a hundred years' time, or so far in advance indeed as we can see?

INFORMATION

The use of money has blinded us with a blanket of other false values. Highly competitive advertising techniques over & above the need to inform & advise have become essential to profit making & if the public reaps any advantage from them it is only incidentally: but this is not really the fault of private enterprise or the advertising industry, for profit-making is a natural feature of any money system. Nevertheless the effects are unfortunate, for instead of factual information which can help us to choose easily & quickly those products most suited to our neeeds, we are bombarded by junk mail often making exaggerated, misleading & deceptively flambuoyant claims, claims to which we have become so accustomed that we are unaware either of their subtle influence or of their frequent stupidity. Advertisers do not always intend to deceive but their claims are seldom more than half truths & even when true are often misleading. One would not accuse Rolls Royce of deliberate misrepresentation if they claimed that their cars were the best in the world but such a claim could be meaningless. Best for what? Best for whom? At what price?

Not only is advertising misleading, however, its inanity & impertinent intrusions, especially on television, are unnecessarily irritating & its insidious subtle indoctrination of materialism & greed into children & those who cannot discriminate, may in the long run prove disastrous. Choice is difficult enough for those who are critical; for those who are not, advertising can become an all-pervading menace. Indoctrination, whether of advertising, religion, the police state, or any other persuasion, however innocent or well meaning it may seem, is so easily accepted that we need forever to be watchful for it & to accept no opinions, including those advocated here, without searching criticism. No belief or organisation is inevitable or true for all time, for as man changes so his universe changes with him & it is only we the enfranchised who can expose such indoctrination & by doing so are able to make continuous adjustment to keep beliefs & changes in focus & in equilibrium. We in Great Britain, however far we may be from complete freedom, are fortunate in that up to now we have had no need to fear that we will be shot for peaceful protest.

Much of the information that we receive today is useless, misleading, unnecessary, often quite ridiculous &, in employing talent that could be put to better use, very wasteful. Can it really be necessary for public - or even private - monopolies to advertise products with which the public is perfectly familiar; must the obsessive degradation of sex or projection of violence into a public prostitution, or the incitement to greed & envy, be the first priorities of our information & entertainment industries? Can we really credit the protestations that newspaper editors are quite indifferent to the feelings & wishes of those who own the papers or of the advertisers, without whose custom they would be unable to remain in business? Is this true freedom? Some advertising would be necessary even in a moneyless society, but to employ it other than for the dissemination of reliable, accurate & up-to-date information would be pointless: & this does not mean that it needs to be less colourful than it is today.

This false sense of values & priorities, this distorting conflict between individual well-being & the demands of a money economy, is reflected along the entire spectrum of our lives. Robbery, being an offence against money, is often dealt with more severely than violence or manslaughter, & it is in terms of cash that we value works of art or even compensation for the mutilation or death of those we love. Self-interested property development desecrates our countryside; & we suspect that corruption, though hidden & protected by libel laws, is rife, that money can still protect the rich & influential even if in theory all men & women are equal before the law.

We judge men & women not by character but by the amount of money they have, by the grandeur of their houses, their cars or their yachts. Money impresses us however much we pretend to despise it & few of us can resist the temptation to show how much of it we have or how we acquired it. To speak of the methods we use to 'make' money as good or bad is meaningless, for none of us can claim to be completely honest, can swear before his own conscience that he has never stolen anything, exceeded the speed limit, or broken any other law.

All such values are relative & if it is the business of business to make all the profit it can, how can we blame business men & shopkeepers for withholding information that might affect their sales adversely or for charging an unnecessary & unjustified little extra here & there when the opportunity has arisen? Aren't we all of us, in effect, doing the same? Don't we, each one of us tend to argue - even if only to ourselves - that the way we get our money is justified, whether it is from business, gambling or a safe salaried job; & surely in a competitive acquisitive society every such argument is valid - even for the criminal?

Money bedevils our economic & social life with conflicts between employers & workers & between different employers & different workers, causing strikes, lockouts, violence & hardship. It makes pyramidal social structures, competition & class war, inevitable. It maintains a complicated & wasteful wages & prices spiral in which no-one is satisfied for long; it renders currency instability & periodic devaluation endemic & long-term international economic co-operation impossible.

There are many other, less important reasons for eliminating money. For example, being small, easily hidden & easily transferable, it is a constant temptation to theft: indeed since most other properties are too bulky to be concealed & transported easily, organised crime could not exist without it. The passing of coins & notes from one dirty hand to another & from one dirty pocket - & the proximity of its dirty hankerchief - to someone else's dirty pocket hankerchief, is revoltingly unhygienic.

Admittedly money can be a satisfaction in itself, for most of us have some miser in us that loves to hoard & count his coins, watch his bank balances grow, or to enjoy a gamble, but it would be difficult to justify any claim that deprivation of the opportunity to hoard or spend or gamble money would be a serious hardship.

Often it is the pace of modern life that is blamed for our ever increasing neuroses & mental illnesses, but usually this pace derives directly from the unnecessary complexities of a society obsessed with the need to acquire money - mainly to keep up with the Joneses.

Lastly party politics as we know it might become irrelevant since all systems, capitalist, socialist & communist are concerned largely with the distribution of money & possessions. Without the perennial conflict over money, political parties might become cooperative & advisory organisations, arbitrating between autonomous local decision-making bodies.

We cannot stand still. Just as the motor car must some day give way to a more efficient mode of travel, so one day our economic & political systems with their inbuilt antagonisms & irrelevancies must give way to a system that discards the inefficiencies of production & distribution & leaves the human race free to replace the obsessive desire for trivia by more rational, more real & more rewarding needs.

. . . .

CHAPTER 8

Waste

There is no doubt that the environment is going to impose constraints upon us all to an extent at present inadequately appreciated. The unfettered consumption of energy & natural resources by the developed world will, if we survive, have to be severely restricted if the less developed countriese are to enjoy what we regard as basic necessities. In other words there will be a surplus of energy & materials not just because we are finding new sources but for the simple reason that, there being a limit to the pollution that the environment can absorb, we shall be unable to use those we have. If we don't control population growth & wasteful consumption of resources, the environment will do it for us.

In other words we must become more efficient, so that basic needs & those technological aids which give us fuller & more satisfying lives can have a wider application, none of which is possible whilst we allow money to create cumulative economic inefficiencies.

Using Francis Hutcheson once again we can define efficiency as the employment of a free society so as to produce the maximum satisfaction for everyone affected.

The organisation of individuals as puppets, whether of the State or any other body, restricts possible progress to the limited channels which that environment allows. It follows therefore that in the long run such organisation, by narrowing the field of human potential, inhibits efficiency. Efficiency therefore, can best be achieved by the free association of individuals organising themselves to eliminate wasteful practices.

We think of our highly complex technological environment as being reasonably efficient, that those who organise & govern it as clever & able people & so they are, but just as learning does not necessarily give us knowledge of life, so cleverness & ability are not necessarily intelligence, & having clever men or women in charge of national affairs does not mean necessarily that they are well organised or particularly efficient.

As has been demonstrated, only a limited proportion of the work force is productively employed. Shopkeepers, accountants, bookmakers, advertisers, rent collectors, insurance agents, cashiers, wages & costs clerks & commercial representatives make little if any tangible contribution to national wealth or individual happiness. We employ large numbers of police, solicitors, lawyers, estate agents & civil servants with the object, in the main, of stopping one half of the population getting its hands on the many possessions of the other, usually more privileged, half. These people produce nothing.

Despite efforts to keep the figures we have used conservative, we have shown that less than 50% of our population is productively employed. But such under-estimates must be cumulative so that the actual adverse effect on our efficiency of having a money system must be much greater & to these must be added those in the manufacturing industries who produce equipment for money- manipulating office workers, such as computers, furniture, or canteen equipment.

In June 1967, 5,000 people were employed in the manufacture of office machinery & 633,000 in paper, printing & publishing, & an overwhelming proportion of these office workers must have been concerned directly or indirectly with money matters. How can a society claim to be funtioning efficiently whilst it carries so many non-productive individuals? Since they provide only for the smooth running of our society as it is at present constituted, surely it is the structure itself that needs changing.

In a moneyless society unemployment as defined here would be almost entirely eliminated. Of course even today not all these would be fully productive for always there would be a nucleus of persons who either physically or mentally were only partially capable, just as today there is a permanent nucleus of people who, perhaps because of their inability to create satisfactory personal relationships or to earn some sort of recognition as individuals in this highly populated, highly competitive money-driven artificial world who are regarded - or regard themselves - as unemployable. In a free environment they too might be able to direct their desires for recognition into non-competitive expressions of natural individual talent & so to realise their full potential.

The inefficiency of money is all about us if we start to look, & not just in days lost in strikes, in bureaucracy & in wasteful, inefficient shopping. How many thousands of silly little lawn mowers are bought each year, how many hours of our time are spent pushing them up & down our lawns every week when one man with one all-purpose mower could do a dozen in the same time? How many people service their own cars or decorate & repair their own houses when skilled men with the right tools could do it more efficiently in half the time?

How many disabled people are prevented from becoming economically productive merely because it is expensive to train them or to provide them with the facilities & atmosphere in which they can train themselves, people who even if they were trained, private enterprise, governments & trade unions, may very understandably, be reluctant to provide sheltered, 'uneconomic' employment for them. Yet a man or woman who has been trained to be no more than half effective can in forty years give the equivalent of twenty years full production.

No one who can produce the simplest useful article should be denied the opportunity of doing so, for apart from the fact that he who is occupied is less likely to need attention than he who is left to deteriorate in idleness, even one useful article produced a year is an economic gain to the community. He who can make an artificial poppy, begging for charity, can also make useful & more decorative things. Surely we can look upon ourselves not just as factors of production, little more than mere animals, but instead as thinking, imagining & concerned entities, co-operative & understanding.

These are not all our inefficiencies however. At week-ends, industries are closed down, & idle machines are wasted machines. Just when we are free to go shopping, shops & post offices are closed. We all flock to the sea or countryside at the same time, only to find there with us what seems to be the entire population of the British Isles, peering at us from the adjacent square yard of beach or through the litter-strewn hedge under which we have set our picnic.

In a moneyless society in which goods would be free, public services could be open for us permanently day & night.

Small firms, at present unable to acquire finance for long-term planning, could acquire up-to-date equipment enabling them to be readjusted or be   replaced by other firms with new ideas, until they too became successful & enlarged.   Voluntary unemployment, industrial misconduct, demarkation disputes & all the petty industrial money quarrels would be irrelevant in a situation where men worked from choice rather than from necessity.

Today too much of our lives is wasted in queueing with sheep-like patience to be served or for buses or trains or hospital care; for prescriptions or aids or nursing help or chiropodists; or for a doctor or consultant to see us: all because our environment is organised for money instead of for our comfort & satisfaction. We can manufacture comfortable cars, tangible, glamorous, instantaneous sources of pleasure, but because building roads & car parks & buses shows no immediate titillating return for our money, their very numbers tend to bring transport to a clogged halt. Money has clouded our imaginations, depriving us of our capacity for co-operative enterprise. Each day as patient bus queues wait, millions of half-empty cars pass them without stopping: is this efficiency? Is it efficient when traffic jams pollute our environment, wear out our cars & waste not only vast quantities of fuel but innumerable hours that could have been devoted to production or pleasure?

When problems become inescapable, normally we try to solve them by putting the clock back instead of forward. We talk of keeping cars out of the towns, illogically believing that men & women accustomed to the comfort & convenience of individual transport will go back to shivering in wind & rain-swept queues for infrequent & unpredictable buses. To provide public transport which could be as convenient & comfortable as travelling individually by car, would, even if ultimately cheaper & more efficient, cost a lot of money that (heaven forfend) might benefit someone else even more than ourselves & would mean giving up those big flashy, noisy toys in which we take such childish, selfish pride & which, as our sacred private property, only exceptionally we need to share with others.

We can travel to the moon but remain incapable of transporting ourselves quickly & in reasonable comfort from one part of a town to another: we can afford to build millions of expensive - quickly rusting - cars but remain incapable of solving our basic social problems. We are tempted to choke the streets to evade parking dues which, because every citizen in every town is taxed in pretty much the same way, are quite unnecessary.

Not only is poverty indisputable proof of social inefficiency but it contributes to that inefficiency, for men & women engrossed in the problem of keeping above the bread line have no time to spare to learn more rewarding skills, nor surplus money to buy tools that will make them more efficient. The intellectual & physical deficiencies that poverty creates also constitute inefficiency, for everyone who is exercising less than his intellectual or physical optimum is an inefficient unit both for his own satisfactions & for those of the community.

Society can never hope to be efficient whilst its members jealously bicker & squabble over their petty pennies or pounds & whilst their lives are plagued by the fear that someone else is getting an advantage that they do not have. They become spiteful if others have subsidies or tax allowances or benefits that they do not have, even if they do not need them, extrapolating such fears into their groupings.

What on earth is gained by charging for public services that are common to every community? What does the jealous bickering & squabbling over other people's pay rises or holidays or income tax reliefs or public services or private perks achieve?. Why envy what others have when organisation & co-operation could make all their advantages available to everyone?

Even science & technology, relatively efficient in themselves, are bogged down by the inefficiencies of the money system. Those operating traditional technologies often fight & delay new methods or inventions because their jobs or profits are at risk. How many managements plan for twenty years - or even for five years - ahead? So long as profits are made now, why should they care about new technologies or about the future? Profits would almost disappear if they made car bodies that do not rust or gadgets that would last a long time. They claim to be worried that such innovations would mean unemployment for the workers & loss of dividends for the shareholders but in a moneyless economy this would be a benefit, not a loss.

Can we pretend to be efficient when, sometimes side by side, we have numbers of small shops all selling the same things &, even if efficiently run, making unnecessary work & occupying unnecessary space?

Is it efficient to achieve shorter working hours only by living at a higher pace? Is it efficient to build ever larger cities so that such shorter working hours as we acquire are wasted in pointless travelling farther & farther to & from our work? Are not our very neuroses inefficient? We are born into a troubled worried world crawling painfully along upon its creaking wheels of brass: in some way or other these worries affect every one of us, so that more & more of us have to seek a refuge from them. In the ten years 1957 to 1967 the number of patients admitted to mental hospitals for the first time increased from 47,500 to 89,000. Is it credible that none of this increase results from worries caused by our man-made, artificial environment?

Most of us fret about whether we have enough money, about losing it, how best to spend it or get value for it or how to keep our balance as we perch precariously on the edge of solvency. Most of us are confused by it or by the lack of it, by its muddles, its complicated useless form-filling, its bills, its pensions, its permits. To get money we need certificates for almost everything, to prove that we have been born or have died, are pregnant, or blind or barmy: & we have to pay for a license for almost everything we have or do, to own a television, to show a film, to drive a car, to marry, to brew or sell drinks, everything in fact except to breathe - & in some countries you have to conform to be allowed to go on doing even that.

You pay heavily for all these privileges, for completing your incomprehensible income-tax form or, even more heavily, for not completing - or wrongly completing or just not comprehending - your incomprehensible income-tax form. Surrounded by every temptation to deceive (for the honest man can pay a high price for his honesty), nevertheless you are penalised if you are caught yielding to that temptation.

Business men demand to be freed of such bureaucratic restrictions but business men are no more honest or dishonest than the rest of us & there comes a time when the customer has to be protected. Business freedom can create its own bureaucracy.

Deceitfully camouflaged & exaggerated by advertisement, many of the things we buy are unsatisfactory. Gambling is frowned upon but at the same time encouraged in the sacred name of freedom (of the money lenders) so that you have to gamble a lifetime's savings (in advance) in the complicated legal casino of real estate merely for the fundamental privilege of having a roof over your head or to make or lose money on the stock exchange. Ours is a world in which debt is condemned but hire-purchase officially approved, in which everything has to be paid for & worried over, from the sinful pleasure of watching people kick a ball about, to the compelling luxury of easing ones bowels in a public lavatory.

It is a world of worry indeed, worry about being fashionable or keeping up with the Joneses; about having real jewels that even experts can barely distinguish from paste; about whether to sell shares or buy them; about whether people think you mean or spendthrift; about whether you tipped too much or too little; about losing anything; about providing for old age, one's widow or even one's funeral; about saving for something, getting promoted, losing one's job; about pushing one's children into a better school than those common people down the road; about being robbed or defrauded; about drifting into petty crime oneself; about the temptation to stake all in one big gamble that might remove ones worries for ever, but seldom does.

Our moralists condemn us for having too little social conscience, too little sense of duty, but in this complicated existence haven't we in fact too many duties, too many laws, most of them unenforceable? Bringing up children used once to be simple & straightforward, a matter of letting them fend for themselves around the house, but society tries to turn us into Frankensteins creating in our own images neurotically competitive little monsters programmed to pursue to success their ever more successful likenesses. Small wonder that some, strained to breaking point, short-circuit suddenly to find themselves stripped bare of every vestige of self-confidence, their individualities crushed, lost in a world transformed, a world that has become unreal, impersonal, mechanical, horrifying & sadistically insane.

We should not wonder that the mental hospitals are full or that drug pushers multiply, but that every one of us does not go mad, born as we are into a world of fear, a world in which we tend to become obsessed with the need to protect ourselves, to insure ourselves against sickness, unemployment, old age, poverty & all the myriad hazards of living - or dying - in a money world.

Our inefficient, wasteful, muddled, ill-organised society creates frustration & neurosis. Our politicians, blinded by their own good intentions, fight each other bitterly over a freedom & an equality in which all claim to believe & which, were it not for the restrictive blinkering of their own prejudices, very often could easily be achieved. Confused by their own belligerent obsessions, individuals turn equality & liberty upside down to suit their own petty privileges & narrow little problems, thinking of equality in terms of income, & forgetting that to be equal men must be free. We claim to be free yet are imprisoned by the restrictive inefficiencies & prejudices with which we administer our resources & sanctify our own ideas, emotions & untouchable privileges & beliefs.

This failure to attain administrative efficiency in a highly sophisticated technological age is calamitous. Even if our leaders are forced to acknowledge that problems exist & find that they cannot quietly brush them back under the carpet, they scratch around for the cheapest & least troublesome means to circumvent protest. Why? Because careful consideration & remedy usually involve the expenditure of money, that ultimate symbol of satisfaction, to be spent as meagrely as the public will accept.

'There is no single panacea for all our ills' is the common cry, the clutching at any excuse for ignoring problems & for doing nothing; yet a hundred symptoms might have a single simple organic cause. It is easier to dismiss ideas as 'utopian' or 'subversive' than to face up to problems & to seek their fundamental causes & their remedies.

Has such a world as this any right to judge us if sometimes we turn our minds inward, away from unwelcome facts? Amidst all the nation's wealth too many women have still to exist on such money as their men care to give them, have still to keep themselves & their children on what is left from a minimum wage after dad's beer & fag money have been taken out, have still to live in sub-human conditions in tenements & bed sits, seething ant-hills of personal drama. Too many break down under all their stresses & strains, driving their husbands in turn to desperation, crime & prison, & thus to become parasitic on an already inefficient society. They become dependent on an endless succession of disapproving bumblebellies, childrens' inspectors, probation officers, pensions officers, welfare workers, & all those who seem to be interfering clever-sticks whose purpose is to watch their every step in case they fail to live up the world's incomprehensible impossible standards.

Ours is a world in which from ignorance or lust for money, man buries the countryside in dark brick sores; it is a world of parasitic, haphazard growth of buildings, transport, noise, confusion, a world in which each year there is more & more to be done in less & less time &, inevitably, more & more hospital beds for more & more neurotics.

It is a distracted, noisy world of shortages & wealth, of hunger & plenty. It is a neurotic overworked, overcrowded, greedy world of petty irritation, a world balanced unsteadily on the border of shrieking mass insanity that every now & then topples over the edge into war. Is this an efficient world?

Can the desire to make such a world more tolerable ever be dangerous or ridiculous; doesn't the danger lie rather in rejecting new ideas merely because they are strange, or in accepting those of other people rather than thinking for oneself? What does it matter if some of these ideas prove impracticable so long as we acquire the habit of thinking - & thinking constructively - for ourselves, & of looking upon new ideas as part of the natural order of things instead of as a threat to our personal privileges? Better to strive for an illusory perfection than to shrug our shoulders at it, muttering 'ridiculous', 'impossible', 'utopian'. Our task might not prove so difficult if we faced up to it. Given freedom, which in itself means the absence of fixed ideas, surely civilization can't go far wrong?

We have to do our own reasoning, groping forward gradually to a less chaotic world. In the past, means of exchange were simple & easily controlled & their effects were predictable, but as they spread from traders to people, populations multiplied & a myriad of individual decisions were needed, so that their complexities increased.

The greater the complexities of systems the greater the potentiality for chaos, predictability becoming less & less reliable. Today external events or macro economic adjustments to the money supply, even if temporarily they achieve alleviation of the exchange problems, only serve to introduce further complexities so that the system increasingly gravitates to total unpredictability.

Chaos in this as in any dynamic system can only be prevented by dispersal of the system itself. Financial anarchy can only be avoided by eliminating money altogether, otherwise all our efforts will tend to be self-negating, for this parasite of society's own conceiving & nurturing now governs its host, growing & weaving itself into a hopelessly inefficient complexity impossible to disentangle. Only when the parasite is eliminated will all the useless, aimless, time-wasting, monotonous, unproductive duties that have grown with it, wither away.

Until that happens however, confusion must persist & the output of any country must continue to be restricted not for lack of potential manpower, skill, knowledge or materials, but for reasons that are entirely financial. Its economic health will continue to be restricted by its existing production limitations, simply because imports have to be paid for by exports. If its resources are poor then money will tend forever to keep it poor.

Our objective then is to find a means of eliminating money & power without having to wait for the long processes of education, mutation or scientific enquiry to mature. Usually the desire for power & the desire for money go hand in hand, for seldom is there power without money or money without power: & yet, surprisingly, there have been few suggestions as to how we might remove either of them. Once the influence of money was taken away however, one incentive at least to seeking power must disappear with it. No doubt power will be sought for itself alone, but once everyone were economically equal & secure, the power seekers would have difficulty in finding alternative means of frightening people into submission.

Long ago we stepped hesitantly from primitive barter into the age of money. Now we must prepare for the final step which sooner or later must take us into the age of environmental control of plenty, an age when production will no longer fluctuate in the changing winds of unpredictable irrelevant external exchange factors, & distribution will have become a routine problem that our computers will be able to take in their stride. Such a step may be completed only when the total elimination, not just of money but of all forms of exchange have been realised. Utopian? Urgent environmental constraints may force this upon us sooner than we think.

Essentially we are concerned not with money but with time & the way we use it, that short time on earth when we can be youthful & useful & happy. How many of us attain more than a trifling satisfaction, a mere molecule of real achievement in the three score years & ten allotted to us? -

& merely staying alive will not increase the sum of human happiness. We are as we are, & of our own era & it is difficult for us to change: but the world needs change, it needs new minds, it needs new ideas, & it needs, when the time comes, that we step aside & make way for them. In the meantime we are entitled to make as much of our short lives as we can & to use them to good purpose, for anything else is waste.

We have nothing to lose by adventurous thinking & adventurous experiment. Selfishness may still remain even after the use of money, the one obstacle to greater achievement & satisfaction, disappears, but inevitably much of it must die from sheer lack of sustenance.

. . . .

Is the elimination of money practicable however?

I believe that it is, indeed that it has to be, that its use, now the one great impediment to the ultimate maturity & long delayed freedom of the human race, not only can be eliminated, but eliminated almost painlessly .

I use this latter condition deliberately, for otherwise any change that appeared to threaten the comfort & privilege of the fortunate would run the gauntlet of their antagonism & their resistance, making survival, let alone maturity, virtually unattainable. Nor are we likely to accept changes designed to eliminate our acknowledged imperfections unless firstly they are practicable, & secondly either present no threat of hardship or, at the very least, reduce losses & discomforts to proportions that our defective social attitudes can accept. In general if changes are not to be resisted they must be seen to be of individual as well as of national advantage.

Once we can bring ourselves to acknowledge that men & women will work for other incentives than money, that most of them would find idleness more frustrating than work, that far from there being a shortage of workers in a moneyless society, employment will be so scarce & so sought after that men & women will be desperate to secure & keep it, then the elimination of money will be quite practicable.

What I suggest - & hope to demonstrate - is not only that

money can be eliminated painlessly but that it can be done in such a way that if at any stage difficulties arose or certain procedures proved impracticable, it could be slowed down as necessary & reviewed without leaving any permanent individual or collective ill-effects.

. . . .

CHAPTER 9

Practicability

Can money be eliminated without disrupting such economic security as we, in whatever country, may have? Impossible? If so it would not be because of the organisational difficulties involved, for man is infinitely ingenious, but because of his propensity for turning a blind eye to problems that appear to threaten his self-interest or, if he does acknowledge them, for failing to face up to them. Even if he does face them he may weaken the chances of reaching agreement on the best action to take by putting his own interests before those of the long term interests of the community - & of himself.

As I have said before, since money tends to gravitate from the many to the few, inevitably it provokes avarice, envy, fear & aggression, so that if money is to be eliminated without provoking the sort of bloody confrontation that money itself perpetuates, it can only be done by our being flexible enough to adapt & to learn to agree among ourselves how it is to be done. This in turn means that we must recognise that it is natural that those who at the time would be enjoying their monetary privileges, would resist having them taken away. To do so without antagonising them seems a pretty formidable task for a society conditioned to believe that self interest must come before communal interest; but would it be so impossible?

It must be emphasised that we are not talking about the immediate present. Today, whether in reality or by some monetary inhibition, goods are scarce, but this cannot last. Science & technology are creating a new world, one in which not only will the present waste of resources have to cease but there will have to be conscious efforts to use them to maximum advantage & to fabricate new ones where this is found to be environmentally advantageous. In other words it will become a world in which the problem will be how best to restrict the use of a surplus of resources & to allocate them according to requirements.

That is why, despite the cynicism, I believe not just that it will happen but that we have no choice but to make it happen. The situation will arise in which the inhibitions & inefficiencies of a money economy can no longer be tolerated, that environmental imperatives will force it upon us. One thing is obvious, whilst money governs our lives there is no possibility whatsoever of our achieving a stable, survivable global society.

One of the most encouraging features of the last few years has been the emergence of the United Nations as a catalyst for peace so that even the major powers, constrained by their financial & economic difficulties, appear to have a genuine desire to reverse the arms race. Once countries can bring themselves also to accept that democratic procedures must apply to States as well as to individuals within those States, & are prepared to accept majority decisions for the sake of planetary survival, even though they conflict with their immediate self-interests, a climate might arise in which the distribution of resources can be regulated according to need, & those means of exchange which inhibit social & economic efficiencies will have become redundant.

The strength of the United Nations lies in a charter which forbids it to interfere in the sovereign rights of individual States. This very factor imposes upon those States the obligation to renounce force & self-interest in favour of democratic consensus. Through its network of world-wide organisations & facilities it could be the means by which the restrictions which the environment will increasingly impose upon our present excesses might be accepted. I believe that the United Nations is the essential & the only means by which the human race can survive & whilst the remainder of this work will be no more than an attempt to demonstrate that it is possible to think positively in terms of the elimination of money, I hope to show at the same time that it must involve global decisions taken by a global forum.

What in fact would be involved? Surely no more than the organisation of production & distribution, & these depend exclusively on LAND, LABOUR & CAPITAL. In other words the transition would not be something mystical, something beyond the mind of man to conceive. It would be a practical matter, a matter that could be tackled merely by concentrating upon the technical problems involved. They might or might not be difficult problems, they might or might not take many years to complete, but essentially they would be organisational problems.

It would of course be necessary to recognise & work upon those resources of which there would by then be a plentiful supply, to investigate the degree to which LAND, i.e. those resources which are the free gifts of nature, such as minerals, soil fertility etc., are or can be made available within the limits of environmental acceptability.

Let us try to imagine what steps a country might have to take if it decided to eliminate money. Great Britain, once again, will be used as our example, since it happens to have many advantages for our purpose. It is small & compact so that distances are short, communication problems not excessive, & changes could be effected simultaneously. It has technical & engineering skills & knowledge not critically less than that of other advanced countries, & being surrounded by water, its insularity allows us to consider it in some degree of isolation.

Let us make an assumption that may seem less fanciful now than it would have done a few years ago, namely that the people of the West had recognised that the increasing demands of developing countries for a share of the worlds resources has made their own profligate use of them a threat to the future of life on the planet. Suppose further that an overwhelming proportion of the people of this country had accepted our premise that money was no longer credible as a means of exchange. What difficulties would the country face if indeed it had the courage to go it alone? Obviously they would be formidable.

It would have to have

1. A strong economy with a large balance of payments surplus, strong enough not just to resist antagonistic external & internal pressures, but to retain the confidence

of the financial world. Exchange controls might have to be imposed.

2. An effective customs & excise department that could deter those who would seek to take goods out of the country illegally.

3. Procedures simple enough to obviate escalating bureaucratic detail.

4. Ensured that foreign trade & confidence abroad could be maintained. If the maintenance of sterling as an external exchange medium were not practicable, conversion to another currency would have to be considered.

Inevitably there would be other enormous difficulties but let us assume that the above conditions at least had been met & that the British Government had decided to procede. How would it go about effecting such a policy?

The government would have recognised that its approach would have to be piecemeal, for sudden change would create chaos. It would need also to be able to evaluate & modify procedures at each step. Since in the initial stages there would still be a money-incentive environment in which the stresses & strains of competitive business might become accentuated by the avaricious opportunism of those who would seek to profit from **any** situation, timing would be crucial.

The order in which the products would be freed would have to be planned carefully, not only in terms of resource availability, but also to ensure that any resistance to the changes could be minimised.

Is this an unlikely scenario for a population conditioned to individual self-assertion? Yes, but let us assume that environmental factors, including perhaps a rise in sea levels, have already made such an impact on world opinion that even our aggressive individualism is being questioned, & proceed as though the elimination of money was indeed possible.

Organisational problems can always be solved if the will is there, but the aim would be to ensure that in the interim period the economic & financial life of the country was not interrupted, that people would go to work as before, & receive wages or profits or dividends as before, & that the effect on their lives would be minimal & painless.

How then to choose those first products to be freed?

The following pages contain no more than an effort to foresee some other problems that might arise &, most emphatically, *are not intended as a blueprint for action.*

In this country we are fortunate in that the basic necessities of life, food, water & fuel are already plentiful, with stable & predictable supply & demand. Since to free new products coming on the market, or those which are expensive, might provoke sudden & disruptive demand, the Government might well decide that those basic items, starting with bread, should be the first to become available without charge.

In all economic transactions there are customers, suppliers, employees & producers. What are likely to be the effects on these of eliminating bread prices?

NECESSITIES.

EFFECT ON THE CUSTOMER.

The immediate effect on the customer would be small, since in this country serious malnutrition has been eliminated &, bread being relatively cheap & in ample supply, the effect on demand of providing it free would be slight. It is obvious that those who from financial necessity have, in the past, had to be economical with bread, might become as wasteful as some of the rest of us, but their numbers, relative to the whole community, would be small & the overall increase in demand would not be likely to present any great difficulty. Everyone would gain by the money value of the number of loaves that he or she would have bought previously & by the increased speed & efficiency of a service in which no money changed hands. There could be incidental advantages & benefits but these will be dealt with later.

EFFECT ON THE SUPPLIER

Since shopkeepers would have no source of income with which to meet their overheads or pay for the bread delivered to them from the baker, they would have to be paid from public funds.

Business profits depend partly on volume of sales & partly on efficiency, & since to reflect these variables accurately would need an enormous & wasteful bureaucracy, it would seem reasonable to disturb the present market system, which is already well organised, as little as possible.

When the retailer received his bread from the baker he would endorse the invoice which would then be sent to an account centre where the computer would compare it with previous accounts & with similar accounts submitted by other retailers, in order to check that it was reasonable.

These claims, to which would be added a profit margin based upon previously agreed average profits, would be paid by the account centre to the retailer out of public funds. The centre would have a month in which to raise an objection, failing which it would be obliged to pay. In other words the retailer would be no worse off than before & his existing incentives to maintain efficiency & service would be retained. Wholesalers would be reimbursed in the same way & would have the advantage of knowing that their accounts would be met regularly & on time.

Basic simplicity is essential to efficient organisation. Here no complications would be involved, no intricate bureaucracy introduced & the shopkeeper or wholesaler would be able to continue to pay all the directors' fees, wages, overheads & profits precisely as he had done before the change - & would always have the right of appeal to arbitration.

EFFECT ON THE STAFF

Today bread is supplied either by door to door delivery, through small general grocery shops or through supermarkets, so that few staff would be made redundant. Those remaining would no longer have to deal with money.

EFFECT ON THE PRODUCER

The baker himself would not be affected & would be able to pay staff & investors as before. In the unlikely event that demand - & so his profits - were reduced, he would be reimbursed out of public funds.

Once the basic necessities of life, bread, water & fuel had been made freely available the Government, using similar procedures, would have to turn its attention to other foodstuffs such as general groceries, but no doubt would feel it wiser not to free greengroceries, which are seasonal & liable to deterioration & to variation is quality, until such time as money was no longer in use.

SEMI–LUXURIES

Once this stage had been completed the Government could turn its attention to less basic & semi-luxury items. Since clothing is not in short supply it might decide that no further payment would be required, firstly for childrens, then for mens & womens clothing. The same transitional principles would apply.

One appreciable effect likely would be an increased demand for higher standards, but since the clothing trade is comprised of large producers & retailers who no longer would be restricted by the need to create ever-changing fashions to maintain sales, it should have no difficulty in adjusting its output or its ability to design clothes to fit the individual figure.

In time it could make arrangements so that if a customer so desired, he or she would be able to sit at home & call up on a monitor, three dimensional images of his or her individual figure, measurements of which would be stored permanently, & clothe that image in a thousand different garments. The eternal trudging from store to store looking for the right style, size, fit , colour & pattern - & above all price - would be a thing of the past. With garments freely available he or she would be able to have a fresh outfit several times a day.

It could be argued that, uninhibited by money, & realising that clothes would be instantly available from the local store, people would be tempted into stocking themselves out with large wardrobes, creating excessive demand.

Is it conceivable however that we will be able to sustain our present acquisitive & profligate habits for ever? Already we are facing problems of planetary survival created by our overuse & wastage of energy & other resources, & once pressures from the poorer nations of the world for higher living standards increase demand, we shall be forced to accept that in a world limited by environmental constraints, industries such as this will, whether we like it or not, have to be rationalised.

There are a number of reasons why in this particular case the problem might not arise. Copies could be stored permanently so that a style that a customer particularly favoured would be available at short notice; clothes could be returned to store where those which were not discarded would be thoroughly cleaned & refurbished &, indistinguishable from new, would be available for reissue.

Again, quality clothes are longer lasting & once it became clear that they had ceased to become a symbol of wealth & would be available at short notice day & night from the local store, a large wardrobe of occasional clothing would be regarded as an encumbrance rather than an asset. As our obsession with personal possessions died out, large houses to contain them, accumulating dust & hard work, equally would become superfluous.

Any shortages would be temporary & once customers appreciated the distinction between 'style' & 'fashion' they would realise that there would be no reason to fear a reduction in standards. Fashion has been the result of producers needing to change styles frequently in order to maintain sales, a process that has tended to be both wasteful & restrictive.

Rushing out to buy consumer durables whilst they remained available would be pointless since eventually these goods would be free & plentiful. If necessary the Government could impose a heavy value-added tax to control any such temporary increased demand. Given computerised payments & accounts, taxation would be automatic, instantaneous & kept in step with expenditure. In other words most likely the problem would solve itself; grabbing for possessions would not be worth the effort.

The freeing of luxuries would require a modified

approach, but in order to consider this it will be necessary for us to digress.

TAXES.

In order that the supplier & those who have been made redundant could be reimbursed from public funds, the Government would have to increase taxes, but since in general the person paying those taxes would have been saved the cost of the article (e.g. the bread) that he would normally have had to buy, he or she would in effect merely have been taking money from one pocket & putting it into another. In the long run only the government would hold money, so that taxation, in effect government income, would have to be permanently above expenditure. Additional taxes also would have to be required to finance the training of those people who had lost their jobs, but these increases would be relatively marginal & being an investment, would have to be accepted. How could they be levied?

It would seem important to relate them directly to the purposes for which they were intended.

To ensure that no one would be worse off (except marginally in individual cases, for nothing would be exact), taxes levied on each individual would be little more than the amount that he or she would have spent on the articles freed. Since individual taxation based on individual acquisition would be impracticable, for to estimate what each individual had had, or would have had, would introduce excessive bureaucracy, the only course would be to work on averages.

Since those who formerly were too poor to pay tax would consume a measure of non-luxury items that they could not otherwise have afforded, they too would, as now, be taxed according to income but they would benefit increasingly as more & more goods were freed. The taxes on the rich would need to be adjusted to take account of the portion of the profits that they would formerly have re-invested, based upon their previous savings, thus providing the government with the means in this interim period, to maintain investment.

Let us recapitulate.

Once necessities & semi-luxuries had been freed the British Government would have the following situation. The customers' expenditures would have been reduced but their resulting savings would have been mopped up in taxes based upon a calculation of average prices. Their situations would have been unchanged except that now their use of money would be minimal. The suppliers would no longer have to charge for their products & would have been given funds by the government to pay employees & producers as before. The producers would receive money from the suppliers & so they too could continue to pay both wages & investors' profits. Investors' profits also would be taxed at source & all taxes adjusted so as to recoup an amount in excess of that which the government would need to pay to suppliers. Gradually as money was eliminated, the balance of national income over expenditure would be increased & adjusted according to experience.

LUXURIES.

Now let us see how the Government might cope with the problems of freeing luxuries.

Since luxury articles would have differing values, to consider them separately would involve massive bureaucratic interference. Although in general, luxuries are articles or amenities which either are permanently in short supply or are expensive in terms of materials & manpower, usually they are no more than superior versions of things commonly available to all. The motor car is considered a luxury, yet most people have a car of some sort & few are heartbroken just because they are unable to afford a Rolls Royce. The yacht is normally considered to be a symbol of wealth but plebeian oarsmen are not above rigging out dinghies with sails.

How then could the Government free these luxuries, bearing in mind that tax additions would have had little effect on the rich, whose purchasing power would have been undiminished & would still have been the controlling factor in deciding which individuals would have luxuries?

It has to be remembered that at this stage we are still concerned to ensure that no-one, however rich, shall be deprived of the advantages that previously he or she had enjoyed. No doubt the poor today in our world of fear, of envy & of class antagonisms, would resist such a suggestion, but we are talking about a situation wherein already both the basic necessities of life & the semi-luxuries have become freely available.

So the Government could assume, as an example, that a luxury item, say a car, was valued (since there would still at this stage be money values) at 100 units & that after taxation incomes were, for the sake of simplicity, held by three sectors of the community; the rich, with 100 units a week, the middle classes, with 10 units a week & the poor, with 1 unit a week.

Perhaps people in all social classes would like to have a new car. The rich would be able to pay to the suppliers, the immediate cost of the car (plus a sum laid down for the eventual mopping up of the money supply), say 120 units. The middle classes, with incomes of 10 units a week would have to wait until all the rich people who wanted cars had been satisfied before they could be considered. They would then have to take their turn according to the amounts that they could afford. The poor, with only 1 unit of income left, would have to wait for the middle class to be satisfied before they too took their turn.

In effect therefore, & until supply & demand were in equilibrium, things would be little different from before, but gradually as money was mopped up & supplies increased, the rich & the middle classes would have reduced differentiation, & the degree & speed with which equilibrium of supply & demand was achieved, & the poor able to have the same goods as the rich, would depend upon everyone's efforts. Those anxious for these luxuries would have a direct incentive to help produce them.

Perhaps the motor car would have been an unfortunate article for the Government to have chosen for the first luxury item to free for there could well have been an immediate upsurge in demand. It is probable however that this would have been less than at first one would have supposed for credit would have ceased to be available & the rep. market would gradually disappear. Then again, since public transport would have been one of the semi-luxuries to have been freed, demand would have switched to it from individual transport, & this in turn would have led to a similar transfer in manufactures .

The Government would still have to decide on an alternative means of allocating priority of distribution of those articles which, because of their novelty or scarcity, could belong only to one person or to a very limited number of people. For such articles coming on to the market, allocation would have to be on the basis of first come first served, with random choice where claims coincided.

I have no doubt that there are those who will be able to seize on many aspects of such policies that would not stand up either to logic or to detailed economic analysis. Happily in order to do so they will at least have had to give the matter some thought, & there has been no other intention than to show that it is possible indeed to think positively of the elimination of money. So let us suppose that the government has, in the main, achieved its objective & try to imagine what difference this might have made to the people of this country.

It is inconceivable that money having become valueless, attitudes would not have changed. Since production of cheap articles needing frequent & wasteful replacement would long have ceased, & shortages eliminated, the craving for acquisition, the undignified scramble for everything on offer, must have begun to die out as people had realised that all would be theirs in turn. As the government could point out, people who were impatient could always volunteer to help produce whatever it was that they wanted.

Some problems, such as competition for flambuoyant symbols of wealth & excellence are likely to have ceased to exist. Already works of art can be copied so exactly that even experts have difficulty in telling which was the original.

Deprived of their money value the originals would have only inspirational creative value & their owners would be unlikely to object to their being displayed for communal appreciation. Works which were just large & showy might well become a nuisance.

OWNERSHIP

Here we come to the very heart of our principle. If we are to stand by it, the right of ownership would have to be sacrosanct. What one had one could keep!

There has been a superficial, outdated & quite unnecessary view that ownership is inconsistent with the idea of equality & that all possessions should revert to the community for redistribution according to need. Doing that however, would involve depriving individuals of all those personal possessions which have become so much a part of their lives, & would mean loss & hardship, & create resistance to otherwise reasonable changes. Even an acute housing problem would not have warranted such drastic policies. In any case such questions would be irrelevant in a moneyless economy.

THE LAW

The government would have had to recognise that many inherited anti-social characteristics would persist, & that it might take several generations before changes in the structure of society would be reflected in radical changes in human behaviour. Even if ultimately the conception of ownership became meaningless & all those laws & precedents that had been based on money as a governing social factor, & in which money had been a subject matter of dispute became obsolete, those laws would need to be retained as a final guarantee that rights would be preserved & disagreements adjudicated.

The tendency to react emotionally to social problems however, has led to a proliferation of laws & regulations to control or restrict individual actions, laws, very often, that could not be enforced. In a radically different social structure in which money did not exist, the anti-social behaviour that had been a logical corollary of an aggressively acquisitive society & the emotional reactions that had resulted from that behaviour, would soon have begun to disappear. With them would have gone the need to impose the restrictions on individual freedoms that had followed.

Once goods had become free &, within environmental limits, available to everyone, & once any articles which were damaged or stolen could be replaced without effort, the reasons for much delinquency would have begun to evaporate. Nevertheless it could not be assumed that the laws necessitated by money, laws concerned with property, with theft & with damage, would also become meaningless & void. A system of laws that had been built up over a thousand years, & by & large had kept obsessive greed - from which all suffered to a greater or less extent - under some sort of control, still would be needed. Since money matters had comprised the bulk of all litigation, laws based on them might rarely be needed, but differences of opinion would still exist for reasons that had nothing to do with money. The rule of law therefore would continue to be needed to deal with ownership & other problems & to be available for situations which could not be foreseen.

The concept of freedom is as fundamental as - & is indivisible from - that of equality, & the law, with all its imperfections, would need to remain its protector. Laws would have to remain valid until such time as the legislature in its wisdom saw fit to remove them. Even though the money age in which learned judgements had been given would disappear, those interpretations would need to remain effective in courts of law. It would be open to Parliament to change or eliminate laws as society changed & they became irrelevant, but until they did, the laws as they stood would have to remain.

The fact that charges might be brought under obscure laws that would have fallen into disuse would not absolve the judiciary from the duty of treating them seriously. If rights of property became largely unnecessary - & in a sense anti-social - the rights themselves would not be any more malignant than before. New generations might deplore their predecessors' preoccupation with the accumulation of goods or money, but they would be reminded that without such preoccupation they might never have learned to organise themselves at all, & they themselves would still be nomadic primitives fending each for himself. If eventually that sense of property faded & disappeared it would be because men & women seldom had need to exercise it, had learned how to live together & to organise their communities without it. That, however, would not absolve them from the duty of examining complaints, of being watchful for injustice, & when they met it dressed in the manner of the past acquisitive age, of applying the wisdom that that age has learned from that experience.

Without liberty, without toleration, without the freedom to pursue ideals in their own ways, people would be less contented, less confident, less hard-working, & more likely to become degenerate animal automatons than happy, useful men & women. If people wished to retain property which under existing laws was rightly theirs, personally or by heredity, there was no reason why the abolition of money should be used as an excuse to take it from them.

HOUSING

Of all rights, at least for most people, the right of property would take precedence. For the British Government there could be no question of depriving anyone of his or her home or homes, however much they had of accommodation in excess of their needs. The objective would not be to have an equitable society but a just, purposeful & efficient society in which the sum of human discontent would decrease. If some people lived in slums & others in mansions it would not, as in a society governed by money, be a question of taking from one to give to the other. Though rich people held a disproportionate share of worldly goods & pleasures, the government's objective would be to increase satisfaction, not to deny it, least of all to deprive people of their existing rights & possessions

Inevitably over the years, large properties & rights of property would tend to become white elephants whose owners had been only too glad to hand them over to the community, but this would be an incidental benefit as privilege, no longer needed, became an anachronism.

Nor would tenancy laws need to be amended. Both landlord & tenant would retain his or her rights & so long as money had value the landlord would continue receiving a return on capital. As the real value of money fell - & the landlord needed the money less & less - most would be only too glad to surrender the burden either to the tenant or to a central authority.

Housing for the poor had been provided by imposing taxes upon reluctant payers or by flattering private individuals into believing that their entitlement to public acclaim, a private halo & an assured eternity, depended on the charity that they could bring themselves to offer. It was not surprising that despite council house building standards having at one time been high, the facilities provided were often the barest minimum & granted only on the most abject supplication. Now the inadequately housed could have choice of type of accommodation & of situation

Unfettered by financial constraints, the British Government would now adopt three principles: that shelter, food & warmth, were basic rights; that shelter should be suited to the needs of the individual; & that the local community rather than central government should be the deciding factor in its provision. The homeless & those in inadequate or unsuitable accommodation would be the first to be considered on the basis of need. Subsequently re-housing would be on the basis of 'first come first served', always of course with the right of legal representation & appeal. The objective, a massive one in such an over-populated country, would be to raise standards.

In the transitional period during which money remained the determining factor, houses would be built as cheaply as possible & many people would still buy their own homes, but as money ceased to have value & the jerry-built privately-owned house disappeared, the conventional box-like house to which the occupier was expected to adapt, would give way to homes designed for the individual. Stone floored, barrack-like flats would be modernised or replaced so as to become as desirable to tenants as houses were to their owners.

Parts would be prefabricated, durable & designed to be taken apart & restructured in a multitude of different layouts to suit subsequent occupiers, thus saving labour & resources but permitting a high degree of sophisticated differentiation.

PRODUCTION & INVESTMENT

The factors of production for any enterprise do not come together immediately or without great difficulty. All encounter a number of constraints such as the building of the factory, its siting, the effects it would have on the local people & on the community at large &, in a money world, the overriding bureaucratic inhibitions of finance.

In the transition period the money not being spent or reinvested (which for individuals would have been pointless since money was to be abolished) would have to be mopped up in taxation, so that demand, production & distribution & the amount of money in circulation, could be stabilised. Investment would have to be undertaken by the government but so long as profits & wages still had to be paid, this would not affect entrepreneurial activity or the co-operation & enthusiasm of management.

After the transitional period however, entrepreneurs would seldom encounter many constraints. Central government would be concerned only with the likely advantage of the enterprise to the general public & the availability of resources. Thereafter, no longer concerned with minimising costs, the entrepreneur would have only to consider which sites were environmentally acceptable, to obtain local & environmental approval, & to recruit labour & resources.

MOTIVATION

The question of work motivation has been dealt with elsewhere but no excuse is offered for returning to it because this will be the prime criticism that will be made against the practicability of a moneyless economy.

In fact the problem would be - indeed already is in this

genesis of an electronic era - one of unemployment, too many people for too few jobs. However much we try to pretend that our aim is full (paid) employment things can never be the same. Redundancies must increase, sometimes drastically. Unemployment benefits & the cost of helping the unemployed to adjust to increased leisure, inevitably must become astronomical. If our figure of 10% of man/woman power employed in manipulating money in the production & distribution industries was indeed a gross underestimate, attempting to relate benefits to wage levels in an interim period would be even more of a problem,

In Part 1 it has been shown that a large proportion, likely to be far in excess of 34% of the working population, would have no function in society, which means that the country would have an escalating problem of surplus rather than of deficiency of man/woman power.

Even today volunteers comprise a large hidden workforce. Is it conceivable that in a situation where there is likely to be well over nine million unemployed, there would be an insufficient number of socially minded individuals to take over from those 18 million who, at present productively employed, might wish to give up their jobs to take up non-productive pursuits. For existing employees, no longer conscious that the interests of the bureaucratic state or private profit-making took precedence over their own, & realising that they would be working voluntarily, slackness & inefficiency would become irrelevant.

No! The very scarcity of work would make it desirable, just as gold once had been. Competition would be for excellence; & in a planet in crisis, competition to produce the most energy & resource efficient articles would be regarded as a natural ambition for all workers in all industries.

In Western societies, idleness during periods of unemployment or sickness tends to reduce confidence, undermining any residual incentive to return to work, sometimes even to take up any other form of activity, & this fear & lack of confidence sometimes resulted in total disablement. In a co-operative rather than an aggressively competitive society this danger, as in pre-industrial local communities, might well become irrelevant; nevertheless there would need to be total dedication to a process of re-establishment that would need to be both piecemeal & gradual, & incentives would need to be positive, energetic, sympathetic, & carefully monitored

The whole production process would have to be revised as the wasteful or over-use of energy & resources became unacceptable & all work that did not require highly sophisticated mental skills became electronically operated. Unemployment levels would become so high that no attempt to create useless jobs, were such a course contemplated, would be sufficient to keep pace with them, & all those moral attitudes that had been attached to the nature of employment or its remunerative or productive associations, would have to be changed.

The concept that people who did not work were layabouts living at the expense of others would become untenable. People would need to have other interests & purposes if the human race, even without its propensity to go to war, was not to destroy itself in the frustration of idleness. It was those who would be able to adjust to an alternative way of life who would have the best chance of survival: the rest would become the new social problem. Individual happiness would depend not only upon knowledge & manual dexterity but upon the capacity to adapt. If some, lacking the motive force of money to which they had been conditioned, chose to ignore the facilities provided, preferring to become a permanent drain on the community, this would have to be accepted - & in an economic sense would no longer matter. It would become imperative to ensure that children who would grow up in a free society would be free of such problems.

The opposite assumption, that the entrepreneur had no other motivation than money, also would have to be jettisoned. Such people, being able to take the wider view, are invaluable in any society, their leadership, ambition, & desire for excellence being a practical complement to theorists. Those aspects of entrepreneurial activity which had been looked upon as anti-social, would, as with all others, be seen to have been products of the environment in which they had had to work, an environment governed by money.

EDUCATION & TRAINING

We in the western world are about to enter an age of leisure. Despite financial constraints, the speed with which machines are taking over human activity is increasing rapidly & even the the expansion of service industries cannot stop the process. Drives for efficiency, though frequently nullified by consequent sub-standard workmanship, only increase it. The unskilled are the most likely to be affected. Those who find themselves unable to adjust to changes in working practices are likely also to be those least able to adapt to idleness.

Such a drastic change in technological development needs an equivalent re-adjustment in educational policies & methods. Growing up in a world in which employment outlets will be contracting & leisure increasing, might be difficult enough for people capable of creative effort. For those in whom long working hours had left little energy for other then apathy & boredom, leisure offers little more than the equally purposeless & frustratingly inadequate pursuit of 'entertainment'.

Such activities or inactivities are likely to become increasingly boring & frustratingly inadequate. For people who are bored, any release even though it takes the form of eruption into spontaneous violence, or a demonstration of impatience of democracy, is likely to be welcomed.

Education & training are expensive in money terms, yet the cost of alleviating the boredom & apathy that increased leisure will bring to those who have never been accustomed to it, will be immeasurably higher than before - & thus more difficult to wring from the taxpayer. No-one is to blame for this. We all are self-considering, if only because ultimately it is we who matter to ourselves. Even those who attempt to practice complete self-abnegation are probably doing no more than exercising self-interest, seeking the approval of their maker or of their fellow men - or of their own egos.

The creation of vast amounts of useless bureaucratic

work or just leaving millions of unemployed standing about at street corners degenerating helplessly into apathy or frustration, sensing that they are an unwanted burden on society, rejected by those more fortunate, solves nothing.

A moneyless society would no longer regard children as an economic drag, their education something to be terminated as soon as the ephemeral educational system felt that it had done its duty, or the elderly as a burden to be brushed under the carpet with a basic pension, but all citizens as potential for a better society. Education would be seen not only as an investment for the nation, & as alleviating the problems that leisure would bring, but as the bloodstream of a full life from birth to death; & those who would effect the process would be those who, becoming redundant, would by learning to teach others in however humble a capacity, solve their own problems.

Children today are reared in a society that on the one hand is idealistic & dogmatic, teaching them the value of self-denial, materially or in personal relationships, but at the same time to be acquisitive & materialistic. No wonder they become confused. Commercial competition, the pressures of a society based on the struggle for money, have made co-operation outside the family - & often within it - difficult, with integrity & trust seldom practicable, honesty rare, & truthfulness difficult. Co-operation & competition have become conflicting concepts.

The Government, accepting that all individuals are guided by personal self-satisfaction, would recognise that a peaceful & satisfying society could only be achieved within an environment in which the collective interests of that society were at the same time individual self-interest, that such collective self-interest could only be achieved co-operatively where an extraneous factor, money, did not create artificial conflicting interests, stifling such capacity for co-operation as had been inherited or acquired. In short the number of individual advantages would have to derive directly from co-operative effort & not by virtue of some symbolic catalyst.

It has been a society in which, directly or indirectly, almost every act has involved the use of money & that use, by its very nature, has become an act of war against ones neighbours. How, in such a society, could co-operative self-interest mean other than a sacrifice of individual self-interest? Just as quarrrelling & violence provoke frustration & retaliation, so the competition for money, the widely held belief that inevitably we must strive against each other to get it & that we can enrich ourselves only at each others expense, has made the raising of social standards a slow, tedious & uncertain process.

Our badly organised world with its conflicting, self-cancelling efforts, rigid with stresses, has lacked all but the most primitive semblance of a common will. In the close family situation in which competition for money has rarely existed, there has been evidence enough surely that alteration of our inherited biological characteristics is not an indispensible prerequisite of co-operation, that toleration, non-violence, unity & trust need no longer be thought of as incompatible with self-interest, & that once the individual selfishess which is inevitable in a money system was removed, it would be possible to teach co-operation as realistic behaviour which is of material as well as of social benefit. Peace & goodwill would no longer be commandments conflicting with every other compulsion.

In the absence of the corruption of human behaviour by money, the Government would be able to introduce courses of social behaviour into early schooling, basing them upon the concept that differences were a natural consequence of human variability, were essential to advancement &, if they were accepted as such, could be solved by discussion & co-operation with others. Freedom of thought, freedom of action, freedom from interference by those others, were the bases of human satisfaction.

As money incentives disappeared the level of production of goods for rapidly evolving material & intellectual satisfactions within environmental tolerances would depend increasingly not only on organisational efficiency but on the ability to re-train for ever more specialised & highly skilled jobs. The unions, their members relieved of monotonous mechanical work & the need to mass-produce throw-away goods to achieve the lowest cost or the greatest profit or output, & of the need to waste their energies on self-negating wage claims, would be able to turn their attention to the work of converting drudgery into satisfying & desirable employment in which their members could take some pride.

So long as the world runs on wheels of money, moral & social education alone can have only limited effect. Without money the denial of some trivial tittilation of the senses would no longer be looked upon by individuals as a major tragedy.

Learning different skills, whether of hand or head, equally would become enjoyable. Young people would no longer be herded together forty or fifty at a time, pushed on to the next age group with little regard to whether or not, (perhaps from fear of teacher or of ridicule), they had missed some vital step. Left to hide rotting & forgotten at the back of the class, often they have been classified then & for the rest of their lives as dullards. Fear wipes clean the blackboard of the mind leaving just a black void of confusion & self-doubt.

Given mechanical & electronic aids to repetition & new methods of presentation, the removal of age barriers would allow the brilliant child to forge ahead at his own speed & it would become evident that the differences between slow & rapid learners would be seen to be of kind rather than of quality. No groups or types have a prerogative of thinkers & philosophers, for every vision of the world, & everyones' imagination, has some value. Only when the desire to know & to excel ceased to be confined to the quick-thinking & successful minority, would the potential of the human race be fully realised.

Where colleges & universities have been just incubators for eggheads, the only barrier to learning would become the individual's own assessment of his potentiality. Too often an elite of philosophers & scientists, immersed in detail have lost sight of the very universe that they have been analysing. The intelligence needed for that wider outlook, that all-embracing concept which would create the next intellectual or psychological revelation are not necessarily the same acute brains that formerly had populated specialist & analytical backwaters. The man in the street also can assimilate facts & theories, & can be made aware of the world of ideas from which previous educational systems have excluded him. Predictable, repeatable & mathematical quantifiability is only a step to the wider world of intuitive, subjective judgement & tacit knowledge.

WORK

If all the year were playing holidays, To sport would be as tedious as to work
(King Henry IV: Part 1)

It is evident that any change to a moneyless economy would have to be gradual, for at first it would operate in an environment in which individuals had been conditioned by the acquisitive individualism of a money economy; for instance, those confronted with an escalation of leisure for example, might suffer from a sudden intoxication of freedom & leave their jobs for long carefree holidays.

For a time the need for everyone to continue working would increase if only because, within environmental constraints, the economy would have to be compensated not only for the anticipated benefits, such as greater freedom from long hours of work or from the mad scrambles to get jobs done quickly, but also for the former under-production inherent in the complicated money system. No doubt everyone could remain fully employed for several years without running out of essential work & it would take this time anyway for attitudes to adjust. The country's needs - & those of the less fortunate parts of the world - would keep many people busy for as long as they cared to be creative.

The argument - made mainly by those who have made the accumulation of money their own motive power - that money is the only real incentive which will make people work (notice the word 'make') & that without such incentive it would be impossible to rely upon them to do so conscientiously, to keep regular hours, or even to turn up at all, is fallacious. Money is *not* the only incentive - or even in most cases the primary reason - why men & women apply themselves creatively. Most of them work because idleness makes them discontented.

Increasingly as automation took over & the number of

people required to provide services was reduced, absenteeism, idleness & demands for shorter hours would cease to be social problems. It would be unlikely that training for leisure pursuits would have had sufficient time to have matured before money was finally eliminated, so that jobs would be at a premium & work regarded as very desirable, instead as formerly of being performed under duress or because of the moral attitude that the (moneyless!) jobless were parasites.

The more communally purposeful work becomes, the more individually desirable also, for all work must have an objective. Merely to occupy oneself or to have an ephemeral interest - in art for instance - would not be enough. Increasingly therefore, new skills would be sought with enthusiasm & the main problem might well be in too intensive competition for those jobs which were available. If idleness were then a problem, it would be in the enforced idleness caused by the inability of mankind to find outlets for the employment of its skills.

Certainly it is not possible to achieve efficiency without discipline for no organisation can function effectively unless its parts can be relied upon, but discipline must be self-imposed, imposed by ones personal desire for work - & for free men in a free society surely no other answer is possible. In these circumstances standards of work inevitably must rise sharply. Where there is no compulsion to work, the only objective will be excellence - otherwise why work? - & this can be competitive excellence.

The greatest threat to human satisfaction is the possibility that work will have become so scarce & its practical & social aspects such an essential need that it would have to be created artificially & purposelessly: & solving the problem would become the criterion by which success or failure was measured. Since individuals have a vast capacity for enquiry, exploration & experiment however, given such variety of aptitude and interest it is impossible to imagine the day when the universe will be so completely explored & understood that we would fail to find anything new to occupy our minds & bodies.

We are not all studious & artistic by temperament, however, able to turn to new arts, crafts or studies: we are not all thinkers or artists.

The trouble with intellectuals, those who think, those who try to look into the future, is that they see life as an extension of themselves - as I suppose, do we all - but there are infinite numbers of ourselves, all with different views of the world.

What will the vast majority of people do with so much leisure? There is a limit to the number of package tours one can take, a limit to places to see, a limit to the number of tele sitcoms, crime & spy yarns, quiz games, sports, & perpetual quarrelling on soap operas, even a limit to the number of sports & pleasant D.I.Y. jobs that we can take part in & do ourselves.

It is O.K. for your intellectual. The world will be his, unlimited enquiry, unlimited interest, a limit only to his time on earth; but what will happen to the rest? Will they all go mad? Will criminals be looking for other crimes to replace those that have become pointless? Will people become so bored eventually that they will exterminate not just themselves but everyone else? Is this perhaps what is already happening to us? Does this mean that we shall have solved the problem of inequality only to have the unemployment problem with us still, only in a different way?

Will we be pleading 'Gi..us a job...I can do that better than him - any job, just to get rid of this dreadful, dreadful nothingness - even to the point of saying 'gi..us our money back?'

What in short, is to happen to those who are just plain practical people?. Are they to be discarded like out-dated cars? I believe that we underestimate ourselves. Individual personality is not only infinitely variable but its potentialities - even those of the school dunce or the dreamer - are virtually untouched (wasn't Winston Churchill something of both? Would we ever have heard of him if he hadn't been of his class?) Even in the age of cleverness that lies ahead there will, I am sure, be a place - even an essential need - for every one of us, for with education still in a formative - indeed barely more than primitive - stage, who can tell what man's potentialities will prove to be? Leisure interests, not just limited to sport or photography or model planes or gardening, can be infinite & will expand as the world expands. Life will be what we make it; what we must learn is how to see that it provides maximum satisfaction.

Centuries of competitive greed & jealousy have conditioned us all to the belief that to qualify for his share of the earth's bounty, a man must bind himself for eight hours a day or more to some unpleasant & frequently purposeless task. I have shown that without money to inhibit efficiency we would have a reserve labour force of thirty four percent at least - in practice it is likely to be well above this figure, indeed if I were foolish enough to stick my neck out I would put it at twice this figure. Some will take up non-productive work or add to the numbers of those who already beautify our environment. Some might just lack the motive power to get off their shoulder blades, but as long as we who work enjoy what we are doing, knowing it to be useful & creative, does it really affect us if those poor souls lack our interests or our ability to mix? Surely the ones whose lives trickle away without achievement deserve our understanding rather than our condemnation.

THE RESULT.

It is difficult to speak of the future without sounding like a visionary theorist, & so to be accused of Utopianism: yet if we cannot change the deplorable past & present, at least the future, exciting, unknown, & with unlimited possibilities, can be ours to shape to our needs & desires. But we must confine ourselves to logical probability when we try to assess some of the consequences of a moneyless society.

The most likely change would be that in general, substandard & 'cheaper' quality goods would disappear, for example all those toys & electrical & mechanical gadgets which break almost as soon as we buy them & which in the long term are uneconomic to produce, irritate the purchaser, give no satisfaction to those who design & make them, waste resources & add to our ever-growing mountains of refuse. They would have no purpose once the competitive need for short term economies or perpetuation of demand was eliminated. Thus it would have become possible by concentration of resources, to achieve economic mass-production of high quality goods, a process that would have made British exports highly competitive.

We have become so accustomed to the petty inconveniences of our environment that we notice them only occasionally or when they have become exceptionally frustrating. How much smoother our lives would be if we did not have to run the gauntlet of the cash register & all the other irritations which shopping provokes. Theft would become pointless once all articles became freely available so that we would be able to keep our shops open permanently without supervision. There would be no incentive to vandalism once goods became so plentiful that losses - & the vandals - could be ignored, for vandalism is a form of self-assertion. All the frustrations of lunch hour, week-end, holiday & evening closing would disappear, for without the need for security, anything that we needed by day or night would be readily available at the nearest store.

No longer would we allow our life supporting forests to be cut down in order to pester us with unwanted leaflets or bills. There would be no more trudging from shop to shop, no more waiting to be served & no more arguments with the retailer: our complaints would be attended to not only because there would be no firm or shopkeeper to suffer a loss of income by satisfying us but also because the people attending to those complaints would be there because they wished to be, not as now because they had to make a living & were afraid of being accused of satisfying the customer at the expense of the firm.

In each small urban area, instead of numbers of inefficient shops, many selling the same things, with limited stocks, poor presentation & lack of information, stores would have on display or quickly & easily identified, there or in the home, & delivered quickly from a central warehouse, every article in production. We would be able to help ourselves to the things we wanted & with each we could be given not as now, reasons why we should have them, which in general we would know already, but details of their limitations, their ingredients (& pollutants if any) & any other facts that we needed, without attempt at evasion or persuasion to buy.

Already information on production & distribution can be linked by computer so that supply & demand can be balanced & temporary shortages in one area replaced from another. Eventually, apart from rare luxuries & new inventions, shortages would not exist & waste would be reduced. Those articles which we buy today even though we know that we shall use them only occasionally - seasonal sports or camping equipment for instance or recordings - we could draw from store when needed & return them for reissue when we had finished with them. Instead of the same pictures hung on our walls for years we would be able to change them whenever we wished.

Redundant office blocks would be available for conversion into housing until such time as they could be replaced by specially designed buildings which then could be as high as we wished. This saving in space, together with the elimination of vast areas of unnecessary small single or double storey shops would release much needed land for housing & parks. Freed from mortgages & the financial stringencies under which local authorities have to operate, we would be able to build our environment to our own needs & satisfactions. Free of speculative estate agents & builders no longer would we be abandoned on some vast urban desert, pushed to the edge of a far flung suburb lacking all modern amenities or imprisoned in some cold, comfortless flat with ones neighbour's nocturnal pleasures embarrassingly audible. Instead of barracks we would build homes, instead of tenement areas we might produce neighbourly communities grouped together, self contained & self governing, for though such communities are not easy to construct even where money is not a governing factor, without its restricting influence inevitably the difficulties must be less acute.

Despite, or perhaps because of, the pressures of commercialism, much advertising today is colourful & attractive, brightening our drab towns, but we could rid ourselves of that which is dull, deceptive, inane, that which is irrelevant, a waste of materials, manpower, artistic ability

& brains. The possibilites for the artist free to bring beauty to our towns would in a moneyless society, be limitless. No longer would our television programmes be interruped every few minutes in order that we may be injected with misleading & brain washing inanities endlessly repeated, nor would competition between channels be interpreted as too often they are, as putting on similar programmes at the same time on so-called alternative channels.

No longer would money-making be the primary purpose of entertainment. No longer would footballers be bought & sold like cattle: no longer would we have to watch sports or entertainments from wind & rain swept slopes when we could we watching them in comfort: no longer would county cricket depend on football pools, golf on snobbery or films on superficial majority tastes.

But these would be merely added comforts. The most important advantages of a moneyless society would arise from there being no need for means tests, or threats to individual living standards as a consequence of sickness, unemployment, old age or misfortune, for the sufferings created by a poverty inevitable in a society geared to ascending spirals of wages & prices, & pensions & prices, & the increasing demands & burdens that they create. Wives, deserted or abused would no longer have to seek some charitable shelter, or find work to get a few extra comforts for their families, or go through all the complicated paraphernalia of seeking maintenance orders or chasing errant husbands or lovers. The temptation to marry for money - & the temptation to get a divorce because of lack of it - would disappear. Charity, that corrupts both the giver & the receiver, would no longer be required.

Free of money worries, of fear of failure in a complicated competitive monetary system, those who lack confidence today would become less troubled & less prone to mental illnesses. The number of crimes would be dramatically reduced - & what profit would there be in pushing drugs?

Finally, we would be able to achieve that knowledge of ourselves which we need before we can understand what makes us behave as we do & how we may achieve the satisfactions that we seek. We cannot hope to learn about the human race merely by observing a few individuals at odd moments in their lives, for mankind is infinitely variable & must be observed in its entirety. We have been unable to collate comprehensive statistical details of human behaviour not only because of the enormous numbers of individuals involved but because we value our privacy above all else, fearing not only for our freedom but even that we may betray our wealth - or lack of it - our individual personalities - & our guilts.

Some of these fears would remain real - & valid: but perhaps we are in consequence of them failing to keep pace with a changed world, for without details such as these, not just of one or two of us but of everyone, how can we hope to obtain statistical evidence on which we cn formulate a valid social science? In time most knowledge & information would be available to everyone through the medium of national computer networks . If we are to include statistical information about individuals, information from registrars, schools, doctors, hospitals, housing departments, welfare workers, solicitors, courts, prisons & all the other organisations & individuals concerned with them & their progress from birth to death, we still must find means of doing so without violating their anonymity, & only in a free & moneyless society where corruption, power & advantage would be meaningless, could this be done.

The most important & essential facet of an affluent moneyless society is that affluence itself will become meaningless.   Our present obsession with personal possession will have become obsolete, indeed an irritant. Here will be the means by which the environment - & the human race - will be able to continue to exist & in which technology & society, hand in hand, will progress beyond the capacity of the human mind today to conceive.

A moneyless society would still leave us with our faults & weaknesses, but one area which leads to their exploitation would be eliminated.

Dare I mention love? Would we have a chance at last to love our neighbours? Would the meek inherit the earth after all?

THE SNAG

A Britain with a moneyless economy, its people truly self-governing at last, living together less selfishly, & its capacity to export no longer depending upon the extent to which it could reduce its wages bills & thus, illogically, its wealth, in order to compete, might lead the world.

As long as the rest of the world maintained its currencies however, it would still have to have an international currency with which to carry out its obligations.

The work ethic which teaches us that the harder we work the more righteous we are, has applied even more forcibly on a global scale, for where money regulates exchange, the more we import the more we have to produce in exports to pay for them, but this, in a world in which production must be limited by what the environment can tolerate, inevitably leads to an uncontrolled escalation of resource consumption - largely, at least in the west, on tittilating trivia.

Great Britain, even with a moneyless internal economy, would be exporting still in order to buy those primary or capital goods needed for manufacturing & those which it could not, or chose not, to produce itself. Individuals however, would have no money with which to buy foreign goods & could only obtain them if the national accounts were sufficiently in the black to enable central government, to allow them some external currency. So once again the more that was produced the greater would be the ability, nationally or individually, to buy any imported goods.

Where exports for the individual producer had had to be financially profitable to enable him to earn enough currency to pay him for his manpower & resource costs, the British economy would not be so restricted. Just as grandma's knitting could increase a family income even though it had taken her an uneconomic number of hours to make, so for Britain every article, however small, made from local materials, & however many man or woman hours it took to produce, would help to maximise national income, whatever the price it fetched abroad.

British salesmen, being able to make it known - truthfully at last - not only that all their goods were of first class quality but that every article sold would be guaranteed by the nation, would be able to outsell their competitors, but this would creat its own difficulties. In other words, desirable though this might seem, it would prove counter productive. Other countrys' exporters, particularly the multinational companies, & international financiers, who depended on their sales & money markets, would be likely to combine to resist such a national advantage, even to the point of demanding that their countries return to arms production or of threatening war. Countries behave in the same way as individuals & as long as those other countries retained money they would remain as greedy, jealous, ambitious, & blind to their long term interests as the individuals of which they were comprised.

Further problems would arise. Once it was known that in Britain everything was free, there would be a gold rush that even Alaska might have envied, with the rest of the world flooding in for the pannings. Customs officers would be unable to cope, tourists, previously welcomed for their foreign exchange, would be unable to use it, for everything would be free. A currency deposit might be imposed according to the proposed length of stay, with stringent penalties for those who had tried to evade the law & to remain, but administration would become so involved & laws so difficult to enforce, for it would have been no use imposing penalties on people who had no money left, that even an enormous bureaucracy, hastily set up, could not have coped: and all the time that their cases were being considered before they could be deported, these intruders would be living on the British economy.

The experiment, as critics would already have foretold, would have been a failure, & if Britain could not have done it, no other country lacking its insularity & compactness, could have hoped to have been successful.

Must we then agree with the cynics, that all this had been wishful thinking?

Not necessarily! The high ideals & the many successes of the United Nations in the area of conflict, demonstrate that in time, where our very survival is seen to be under threat, public opinion can be persuaded, & can persuade governments, to look beyond their own narrow national interests & bigotries.

The possibilities for the United Nations in this process are limitless, not just in collating information & allocating & limiting distribution of products, but in providing information & facilities for research & production. In a moneyless society there would be no unnecessary restriction on output, agricultural or otherwise, whilst millions starved or lacked the basic necessities of life, merely because they had no money.

Let us be clear however. The objective always must be less government, not more. MAN must learn to govern himself. If the U.N. has, in the interim period, to be the catalyst by which money becomes redundant, it must never become a world government.

Macro & micro social & economic organisations need not be incompatible. Without the distorting individualisms essential to a world of money, each must have its place, the U.N. providing for planetary problems within which continental conglomerates can organise inter-state needs, & individual governments providing the facilities for those of individual counties or cities, but ultimately the smallest unit, the tiniest village or urban unit, is the most efficient, for it alone can know what it can best produce. Governments, however large or small will have to learn to confine themselves to assessing areas of need, to advise & help in regulating production & growth, & to organising distribution.

Here too in the smallest communities it may be found that money will be most reluctant to leave the stage. Difficult though may be the process of eliminating money from the world of high finance, it is there that money has become hopelessly inefficient, outdated & obstructive to civilised society & where its edifice must first crumble. In far off places where barter first started, & where money could well remain necessary & efficient, may be where its use will last be seen.

Epilogue

Revolutionaries & reformers tend to delude themselves into believing that their ideas alone are sufficient to solve the problems of the world & that given such ideas individual personalities could be changed overnight, but the human animal has made little effort to curb its aggressive tendencies since it started to call itself civilised, so that it would seem reasonable to assume as inevitable that any such changes must take many generations.

Here we are up against a dilemma, for it is evident that man's power of destruction & the attitude of mind of some of his leaders are such that time is running out & that rapid social changes are essential if the human race is to survive. Those of us who live in the western world are fortunate in being relatively rich & well fed, but for how long shall we be able to cling to these privileges? If our outdated & irrelevant attitudes & the increasing stresses & strains of technological change are not to plunge us into a cataclysm, we have no choice but to change the structure of our societies so that aggressive attitudes are either eliminated or, at least, denied anti-social outlets.

A lot of us tend to sneer at social change, to claim that man is evil & aggressive by nature & cannot change. If this is so then as a species he appears to be unique & the final holocaust cannot long be delayed; indeed it is strange surely that he has not exterminated himself long before now. If, however, man himself is not malformed, perhaps it is the society which he has built up around him.

To change the structure of society however, is a massive undertaking; to do so in the short space of time which our capacity for self-destruction now leaves us, requires a complete change of attitude. To go on as we have been accustomed to do, patching up our financial structures in accordance with the current economic theory or as circumstances compel us, is no longer enough. The capacity for mass annihilation is now becoming so universal that there is too little time to make small casual random financial or political changes in the hope that eventually the world will erect around us a shelter of peace without disturbing the comfort of our escapism. If we want to exist at all - or we want our children to exist at all - we must learn to take charge of our environment so that liberty & equality become an inescapable part of it. Only if we can face up to the danger of universal annihilation are we likely to be stimulated to conceive ways by which it may be avoided. Then perhaps, like most such changes, we shall discover that they were far less to be feared than we had imagined.

Society has reached a watershed: its further advance must depend on the extent to which we are prepared to re-examine our assumptions & attitudes & to acknowledge in particular that our affluence, if we have it, makes our obsession with conflict, personal or political, whether for necessities or luxuries, a waste of energy & talents.

From now on either we must accept theories based upon the concept that man is no more than an aggressive acquisitive animal & that he can be assumed to react to an unchanging environment in a roughly predictable pre-ordained manner or we raise our heads & learn that we must so adjust - & adjust to - that environment that we can live & work together. We must accept that we are not just factors of production like LAND & CAPITAL, but worthy masters & servants of the world & its inhabitants, thinking, imaginative, & above all co-operative, understanding & concerned entities able to treat that larger factor of production, the environment, with respect.

We are failing to organise a rich & bountiful world, have allowed food to be wasted whilst millions were hungry, have watched whilst those who most needed homes - & could themselves have built them - have lounged helplessly upon street corners unable to find employment for their hands; have seen shops overstocked with gadgets that would have taken the drudgery out of our lives but that too many of us haven't been able to afford: & we are all responsible so long as we fail to make the effort to overhaul all the basic ideas & beliefs within which such anomalies have grown. Our little dishonesties have grown in & upon us gradually until they have become part of our behaviour. In the midst of plenty wherein greed should be meaningless, most of us are as conditioned to it today as ever we have been.

Smugly we have boasted of our democracy as we have distorted & debased it. We have tied ourselves to a confused, old-fashioned & unwieldy money system, to an obsession with personal property & possessions that by its nature grows upon itself, distorting our natural concern with self into restrictive individual selfishness, worrying about how we can acquire the things that other people have, things that if we stopped to think about them, we probably did not need at all? Perhaps the only people who are secure are those few who, despite discomforts or deprivations, are content to become detached from these pressures &, if necessary, to remain on the bottom rung of the social ladder. For everyone else a standard lower than that to which they have been accustomed or to which they have aspired, is dreaded hardship. Each of us demands his own car, his own bicycle, his own refigerator, his own vacuum cleaner, things some of which we need so very occasionally.

Naturally we would wish not only to secure basic necessities & to maintain our standard of living, but continually to attain a better quality of life; unfortunately we have been conditioned to the belief that the progress & efficiency needed to achieve these aims depends on money incentives, held, in particular, by the sort of people for whom money is the prime incentive, & these, by their materialistic success, are usually respected & listened to.

Need we accept such a low estimate of our motives? What of the other incentives, loyalty, satisfaction, pride in a job well done, interest in the job itself, the respect of our fellows, the desire to please, have we no faith in these, need we indeed take such a cynical view of them? Does not this cynicism derive perhaps from seeing them only as they are affected in, & in conflict with, the money incentive itself? Yet even against this seductive competition, these other incentives have never entirely been eliminated, & without that distraction, of what might their stimulus not be capable?

Even in a moneyless society, these alternative incentives would only flourish if the conditions were favourable. It would be useless & unnecessary for example to try, as we do now, to tailor men to jobs for which they have no natural aptitude or desire. True, jobs would still have to be taught; true too that most would still require courage & tenacity of purpose; but given a favourable environment we can all acquire such qualities: indeed without difficulties & problems few of us could find satisfaction or pride in our work. To use their need of money to coerce men into work for which they are intellectually, temperamentally & emotionally unsuited, is not only inhumane but in the long term productively inefficient.

Today even where there seems to be no financial gain, men & women often become involved in their work to the extent of devising new ideas on which their firms can improve output. Often what inhibits such ideas is the cost of applying them, sometimes leading to complaints that other countries are left to reap the benefits.

To what extent does the desire for money motivate our aggression? Warfare can be the product not only of nationalism, religion, ambition or power but of money too & too often money becomes the fuse. Even if arms were produced still, sales pressures either by arms manufacturers or governments would no longer be a factor.

The elimination of money will not achieve Utopia, for human beings seem to have a facility for finding other means of exercising their residual envy, greed & aggression: but they will be hard pressed indeed to find enough anti-social attitudes to compensate for those that will have disappeared. Emotional & personal problems & organisational difficulties will remain. Problems will arise **because** there is no money, but they will tend to become statistical & organisational rather than competitive social problems. If the elimination of money brings its own difficulties those are likely to be trivial compared with the enormous number that will have disappeared. It would be difficult to   imagine anything more chaotic, unpredictable & absurdly inefficient than the world's stock markets

The social mechanisms of the world of men must be made to work. The past is an inheritance to be built upon, not to be lived in, & if mankind is to survive it must find a way out of the impasse of outmoded ideas.   Whilst inequalities exist, the struggle to eliminate them will continue, yet, as we have shown, it is futile to believe that we can achieve equality of incomes & the stable society that that would bring, merely by adjusting wages, profits & pensions. How much longer are we to go round in circles chasing our ever disappearing tails? What possible excuse can there be for refusing to seek other means of living together?

Let us create a world in which we need no longer promote artificial demand by turning out a lot of surplus or inefficient products or by persuading every family to have one - or two - of everything, things perhaps that they would use but once a week or month or year or lifetime. Today, property rights being sacred, most of us, consciously or otherwise, feel the urge to acquire our own copy of everything, however ephemeral our interest in it & however much trouble we may have to take either to acquire it or if we do not want it to be left on our hands, to go through the complicated process of selling it again.

We have become masters of the art of wasting effort, of frittering away millions of man & woman hours every day - & vast quantities of materials & fuel - not only in travelling to & from stores, works, hospitals, offices & schools, but in building cars & bicycles & buses to carry us. We produce trash that we know will not last, stockings that ladder, cars & artefacts designed for a limited life, flimsy breakable toys, pots & pans that are inefficient & virtually useless when we buy them, & steel tools too soft to do their jobs; & every increase in our efficiency we offset in part by creating more jobs & more laws & regulations for more civil servants, & more lawyers & police to see that they are kept.

Perhaps the most pernicious of money's inefficiencies lies in its creation of bureaucracies. In one way or another most of us love power over others & easily find reasons to create bureaucratic structures to limit freedom. Both capitalism & communism are confined in their own catch 22 situations. The more freedom capitalism gives to the use of money to create private enterprise the more bureaucracy it needs to limit abuse. The more communism tries to eliminate profits from enterprise the more bureaucracy it needs to take its place. Whereever there is money, bureaucracy is needed to control its excesses or deficiencies.

Money, by its nature, can never be completely controlled. Man imagines that he controls money, but it is money that controls man.

Surely it is not beyond us to foresee - & create - a freely organised world of self-contained communities built to meet our needs instead as now, to match our pockets, a world in which man no longer regards the motor car as his most sacred possession, in which transport, no longer individually owned, can thereby be so organised not only to be completely safe but to be as immediately available to everyone as is a car to its owner today.

In a moneyless society the media, newspapers or television or their equivalent would provide information & entertainment only, for pressure advertising would be replaced by facts, profit making incentives by a desire to present those facts with skill; & every one of us, even we who are never heard, who never become local big-wigs or public figures, would have the right & the means to air our views instead as now of having to trust to the availability of time, space or a sympathetic editor.

Not too far away, if the human race survives, is the end of a long journey that has taken us from the single minded individuality of the club-wielding cave man, through barter, simple coin swopping & high finance, to a means of exchange that is completely simple, completely fair, & can become completely efficient. Only when the creaking money god is dead shall we be free, free to control our production or our hours of leisure, free to be our own masters. With peak demands adequately met with minimum affort, & high quality goods available that will last, probably, until new inventions or ideas make them out of date, we will have freed ourselves from the need to organise for protection against each other. With those who work free & self-organising, there will be no wages to fight over or to strike for.

In a moneyless society there would be worries enough, but at least the struggle for existence would not be one of them. It would no longer be every man for himself, the survival of those least fit ethically to survive, the aggressive, the crafty, the knavish, the anti-social, all the sharp-witted extroverts who make for strain & insecurity: as the conditions that created such attitudes became obsolete, the species would die out.

All the endless complications involved in the simplest process of organisation would be thrown aside, the bargaining over costs, over hiring or buying, the complexities of estimating vaguely the relative values of artefacts, of individual skills & of individual effort, of overtime, Sunday time, piece work or job contract, leading too often to enervating, profitless disputes & law suits, man putting a price upon man, degrading him to mere merchandise, & to become in consequence petty, mean minded & unco-operative.

Gone will be the endless striving, the temptation to change our job to one we hate so as to get a larger slice of the cake, & having in consequence to accept endless, pointless, ulcer-creating worry.

Our freedom must become real. Today we can barely step from our doors without breaking some law or other, failing to return our library book or walking out of a store without paying for our goods, laws based on the assumption that we are automatons programmed to have criminal tendencies instead of being full of imperfections, forgetful, worried, nervous, & fallible, with a tendency to day-dream at the wrong moment, laws so numerous that if it were not for the unwritten acknowledgement that we all break them, each of us would need an individual computer to avoid perpetual penalties. Yet invariably our remedy is to impose more & yet more laws, each needing individual interpretation until even our lawyers tend to get lost in the legal maze & our claim to liberty becomes a farce.

Even if in the long run it would prove to be cheaper to try to create conditions in which the misdemeanours cannot happen & the laws become unnecessary, we try it, if at all, only as a last resort. Our first concern nearly always is the immediate problem, usually the security of our purse strings. We endure all these petty laws & restrictions because we believe that they protect us & enable us to live together amicably, failing to recognise that every law, however necessary, is a restriction of liberty & a confession of failure. Too many of them fashion us to our environment instead of fashioning our environment to suit our needs. Better, surely, to ascertain the root causes of our organisational deficiencies & to attempt to remove them, before we start to overload them still further with restricting regulations.

Restrictions - dictatorial or otherwise - do not solve muddled problems, only add complications to existing confusions. The more laws we make the less of them we understand &, as learned minds try to interpret them, the greater our disorder, making us seek further laws or precedents to clarify the old ones. The more laws the more muddles & the more muddles the more laws. Simplicity is the basis of efficient organisation &, in consequence, becomes the essential basis of freedom.

Perhaps the greatest boon that the abolition of money would bring would be that the laws that money has made necessary, laws on larceny, prostitution, maintenance, robbery & fraud would become obsolete - & this wouldn't seem to leave a tremendous number to worry about!

Our freedoms are restricted by our own limited horizons, tempting us always to impose restraint upon those whose beliefs differ from our own.

Liberty is like truth, too delicately poised to be tampered with. Just as telling lies starts with subtle evasions & progresses by way of little fibs to a life built upon the shifting sands of deceit, so coercion is cumulative. Restrictions - & we are all adept at making excuses for restricting people of whom we disapprove - lead to controls & controls become repression until we wake to find ourselves imprisoned in a cocoon woven of tiny strands of our own devising.

We have tended to confuse freedom with possession, to think of the denial of material non-essentials as a denial of freedom. It is not! There is a threshold of sufficiency beyond which freedom becomes self-indulgence acquired at the expense of ecological limitations. We tend to apply our vague sense of the value of liberty to selfish ends, concerned too often with preserving our monetary rights, gradually winding controls & repressions about ourselves without noticing it. Money is power & we cannot repeat too often not only that power tends to corrupt but that freedom must be made as full & complete as the circumstances in which we find ourselves - that we can control those circumstances.

Full & complete! One is tempted to leave it at that & make a nice tidy scientific sounding law ending with a full stop. Unfortunately there must be one exception, one freedom that we must deny ourselves, & that is the freedom to interfere with others. Essentially freedom means physical freedom, freedom from interference by another. This, as already shown, is not to suggest that physical interference is the only misuse of power, but given physical & economic freedoms most other powers should tend to wither & die.

Men & women should be free just as long as they permit others to be free. Only if they interfere with others, whether physically or by imposing their wills upon them, should there be any question of taking their liberties from them.

Freedom is paramount! Violence is a denial of that freedom & is never justified in a democracy & only rarely if at all against a dictatorship, for usually any benefits it might achieve are cancelled out by the violence it provokes. This is not necessarily to condone non-resistance, for violence leads to instability & if we wish for a stable society we must resist violence. Indeed to be practical, how many of us would not protect our families if they were attacked; but the necessity to protect our homes or our homelands does not permit us to invade others or impose our ideologies upon them, nor does our indignation at injustice warrant our using violence to correct it, except as a defence against violence itself. Nor can one extrapolate automatically from the individual to the communal. Because we are justified in resisting a personal attack, that does not necessarily justify our going to war to maintain the status quo or to satisfy some emotional reaction.

It will be argued that complete freedom would bring anarchy, an excuse for universal self indulgence, or for giving too much freedom to other people: you & I are different of course, intelligent, capable of self-control, of adjusting ourselves to new conditions, but what on earth would happen if all those lesser beings who need the guidance of our superior morality & intelligence were free to become corrupted by films or books or plays - or freedom?

Criticism is always self defeating in the long run. None of us likes to be judged & for the most part moralising, like using force, only creates an opposite reaction. Ethical opinions are but value judgements & too often lead us to confuse that which is wrong in our view from that which is mistaken. Hitler & Stalin imagined that their actions were in the long-term interests of their nations. We think that they were mistaken.

Are the dangers from freedom - if they exist - greater than those we have already, or is it just that we fear for the sanctity of our own privileges? Can there ever be too much freedom? Surely experience suggests that to interfere with personal liberty is to let in all the evils of power: & he who wields power, demanding that others shall obey him, even in the name of God, is creating God in his own image. Isn't this to deny freedom - & God - altogether?

Liberty, once it ceased to be the prisoner of our predatory money lusts & all the parasitic bureaucrats that are needed to curb them, must no longer be restricted to habeas corpus or the right to make profits, but become a reality. One day perhaps we will no longer have to submit to the beliefs & moralities of others, will discover that we need no longer make unacceptable sacrifices to attain a better way of life, will learn that that which is desirable, however remote or improbable it may seem, is always worth striving for so long as it doesn't harm others, that our present limited knowledge gives us no reason for believing that any of our goals are unattainable & that even the political problems at which we gape so vacuously can be solved.

We have within our grasp a freedom hitherto only dreamed of, a freedom that will be denied to no one but he or she who seeks to deny it to others. Once man's fallibility is no longer exposed to the corrupting influence of money, power - the ability to dictate to others - will become as obsolete as money itself.

Since each of our millions of body cells possesses a number of different possibilities, we cannot help but be infinitely variable, & unless we permit our scientists to manipulate those cells otherwise, that variability is also a guarantee against permanent dictatorship of the human race. As yet we are too complex to conform to the mould into which our masters would try to force us; & once we achieve freedom, real freedom, & that threat disappears forever, our potentialities seem limitless. If today, mass educated though we are, our individuality still can blossom forth in limitless variation, what might not it achieve when it is released at last from the limitations which greed, money lust & selfishness impose upon it.

Liberty has still to evolve, is still only a vague generalisation veiled by a multitude of beliefs & preconceptions. All beliefs whether political, nationalist or religious, are potential tyranny, for each claims its own to be the only true belief & regards its rivals as depraved & corrupting myths upon which moral sanctions & physical restrictions may justifiably be imposed. If ideas & ideals bring out the best in men & women they tend to bring out the worst also, war for instance, intolerance, or hatred, for we fail to see that high ideals often are reflections of our own vanities, vanities that debase the ideals themselves. If our beliefs cannot face criticism & enquiry, cannot live upon their own merits, surely they themselves must be suspect. If vaunted & obligatory virtues such as work, patriotism, chastity, martyrdom, courage, must flourish at all it must be in their own right as free expressions of individual personality. Every moral imposition, whatever the motive, is potential tyranny.

One day perhaps, freed of the stresses & passions of greed of money, our democracy, renewing itself at last, may well look back upon restrictive government as a barbarous relic of the embryonic age of man.

Before it can do this however, it must create a society in which the people can govern themselves. Differences of opinion are necessary & will always exist but if the struggle for money, the greatest single factor contributing to dissention & strife were eliminated, at least our differences might be contained within a peaceful context. Only when we recognise that power & organisation are separate & distinct functions & we have created conditions in which society may be organised for the maximum satisfaction of all, will power - & governments wielding power - become superfluous. If society without government is anarchy & we associate anarchy with violence, perhaps we - & the anarchists - should re-examine our attitudes.

Today those who behave irresponsibly do so perhaps because they are regarded as such but mainly because they are conditioned to an environment that is unequal & lacks all but the most basic of freedoms.

Liberty & equality are like mass & energy, different in kind but interchangeable, & each must be complete.

A secure, peaceful & co-operative world wherein men & women are free from the constricting wastefulness of feeble, useless tasks, a purposeful world in which men & women can work freely at their own pace & in their own time, is almost beyond our comprehension, let alone our achieving. It is too easy to accept without question the smug belief that in essence society cannot change, that human nature is fixed & immutable.

We have no choice. Either we become intellectually adaptable & survive or we remain socially aggressive animals, in which case we shall die out with them.

For the last two or three thousand years we have accepted that individual personalities brought up to competitive greed & jealousy can be transformed by denunciation, precept or example alone, but the results justify us in questioning whether in the time in which the environment will still permit us to exist, such a transformation is likely to take place.

We cannot claim that our efforts to adjust to the technological twentieth century have been a great success.

The electronic/biological third millenium is almost upon us & we lack even the vaguest idea of where it is taking us, let alone that we could take charge of it & mould it to our own needs & to those of the other inhabitants of the planet to whom we owe so much.

Over this long period most of the satisfactions of mankind have been the prerogative of the fortunate, the unimaginative, the belligerent, the ambitious, the selfish & the extrovert. We have reached the evolutionary stage when we should be able to ensure a full life also for the unlucky, the weak, the meek, the timid, the thoughtful, the inadequate, the gentle, the quiet, the unprotected, the needy, the sick, the frail, the backward, the slow of understanding, the persecuted, the peacemakers, the poor in spirit - in other words for all of us.

APPENDIX A

RAIL PASSENGERS.

In 1986 railways carried 30.8 bpk (billion passenger kilometres) on 14,304 km^{TS} (of route open to passenger traffic i.e. 2366 km less) of normally 2 way rail, i.e. approximately 2.15 million passengers per route kilometre. Thus with 32,464 kms of route, there would have been 69.80 bpk. But inter-city lines carry 165 passengers per train as against an average of only 100 passengers per train, so on the new lines an extra 5.18 bpk could have been carried, making a total of 74.98 bpk, i.e. 44.18 bpk more than in 1986.

ROAD PASSENGERS.

Roads carried 475 bpk on 350,407 km^{TS} of normally 3 lane route (only 5,450 km. i.e. 1.56% being of dual carriageway), i.e. approx. 1.36 million passengers per kilometre of which :-

Motorways.

Cars & taxis travelled 31.82 bvk carrying an average of 1.85 passengers per car, i.e. about 58.87 billion passengers, whilst buses & coaches travelled 0.34 bvk carrying an average of 13 passengers each, i.e. about 4.42 billion passengers, a grand total of 63.29 billion passengers on 2,968 km of route (mostly 6 lane) i.e. approx. 21.32 million passengers per kilometre ^{TS} We would have lost 1,484 km of motorway at a rate of 21.32 million passengers per kilometre i.e. 31.64 billion passenger kilometres, leaving a total of 475 - 31.64 = 443.36.

Thus there would have been a nett gain overall in PASSENGER traffic road & rail of 44.18 - 31.64 = 12.54 bpk or 2.48%.

APPENDIX B

RAIL FREIGHT.

In 1986 railways carried 16.5 btk (billion tonne kilometres)[TS] on 16,670 km [AAS]of rail, i.e. approx. 0.99 million tonnes/k. Assuming again the same average use, our 34,830 kilometres of rail would be carrying 34,830 x 0.99 or 34.48 billion tonne kilometres. But this again is an average. Assuming the same efficiency as inter-city passenger transport, high speed freight on new lines might well increase their carrying by 0.65 i.e. 3710 x 0.99 x 0.65 or 2.39 btk. giving a total of 34.48 + 2.39 = 36.87 btk.

ROAD FREIGHT.

104.1 btk were carried on 350,407 km [TS]of road, i.e. approx. 0.30 million tonnes/k. of which :-

Motorways
Motorways carried 14.8 btk [TS]on 2,986 km of road i.e. approx. 4.96 million tonnes/k. Thus there would be a loss of 1,484 km of motorway at a rate of 4.96 million tonne kilometre or 7.36 btk. a total of 104.1 - 7.36 = 96.74 giving a nett increase overall, road & rail of 13.01 btk., i.e. 10.79p%.

APPENDIX C

ENERGY CONSUMPTION.

Road transport energy consumption in 1986 was some thirty times heavier than by rail, 12,944 million therms for 350,407 km of track i.e. 36.94 million therms per 1000 km as against 424 million for 16,670 km i.e. 25.43 million therms per 1000 km [TS]. Energy saving on roads if there were only 1484 km of motorway would be 54.82 million therms, whilst increasing the railway mileage by 18,160 km to 34,830 km, would cost an extra 462 million therms, a nett increase of approximately 407 million therms or 3.04%, assuming that relative fuel consumptions motorway/all road :H.S.train/all trains are approximately the same.

APPENDIX D

ACCIDENTS.

3.   Road casualties in 1986 numbered 321,451, (with motorways 5,162) as against 511 (movement only) by rail, [TS]. This was an exceptionally high figure for rail, rating 14.4/ bpk as against an average of 10.6/ bpk.

A reduction by half in motorway construction would have saved 2,580 injuries a year on the roads but to have retained our original railways & added a further 3,710 km, giving an additional 18,160 km of route, would have increased rail casualties by 557, a nett decrease overall of 2023 or 0.63%.

APPENDIX E

ROAD TRANSPORT

MAN/WOMAN POWER EMPLOYED.

Production of motor vehicles & parts.	252,000
Repair of motor vehicles & parts.	204,000
Wholesale distribution & repairs.	1,184,000
Retail distribution motor vehicles & parts, filling stations.	230,000
Road passenger	192,000
Road haulage.	232,000
Total.	2,294,00

Other road passenger transport, miscellaneous & supporting services, ie 248,000 have been ignored since they appear to include other forms of transport.

Index

Ability, 82–4
Accounts, National 44
Advertising, 84–5
Ambition, 72
Anarchy, 146
Artificial Intelligence, 49

Bigotry, 6
Bureaucracy, 19, 93 et seq, 140

CAPITAL, 6, 13–9, 26–7, 48–9,
    103, 136
Capitalism, 6, 9, 10, 87, 140
Censorship, 78
Communism, 6, 9, 10, 79, 87, 140
Competition, 65 et seq, 118
Customer, The 105

Defence, 5–7, 9, 16, 43
Demand, 15–6
Dictatorship, 6, 9, 62, 78–9
Disablement 54
Discipline, 125
Drugs, 51

Ecology, 50
Economics, 13–16, 26, 47–8, 136
Education & Training, 71–2, 120
    et seq,
Efficiency, 10, 11, 37, 79, 88
    et seq., 95–6
Electronics, 49
Employees, The 106
Employment, 89–90, 117–9
Energy, 49
Entrepreneur, 119

Environment, 7, 49–50, 58, 65
Equality, 61–5, 82–3, 95
Experts, 62

Financial Services, 5, 45
Food, 50–1, 54
Forests, 50
Freedom, 78–9, 95, 114–5, 122,
    141 et seq,

Growth, 58

Health, 52, 54, 58, 95
Heredity, 9, 65
Homelessness, 54
Housing, 53–4, 115–7, 129
Hutcheson, Francis 60, 88

Idleness, 120, 125
Incentives, 48–9, 67 et seq.,
    120 et seq., 138
Indoctrination, 84 et seq,
Information, 84 et seq,
Inhibitions, Financial, 66
Intellectuals, 125–6
Investment, 14, 45–6, 117

LABOUR, 13–7, 26, 42–3, 48–9, 103
LAND, 13–7, 26, 42–3, 48–9, 103,
    136
Law, 39 et seq., 95, 113–5, 141
    et seq,
Leadership, 72
Leisure, 67 et seq., 120 et seq,
Liberty, 61–3, 78–9, 95, 114–5
    122, 141 et seq,

Luxuries, 110–2
  Semi-, 107–9

Manpower, 42–6, 56–9, *& see
  Transport*
Marx, Karl 7, 61
Mental Health, 55, 58, 87, 93–7
Morality, 6–7, 16, 48, 69, 95, 119,
  125
Motivation, 48, 71–5, 117–9

National Accounts, 44
Nationalisation, 17–8
Necessities, 105–7

Oblomov, 67
Organisation, 77
Ownership, 113

Quality, 127

Politics, Party 87
Pollution, 6, 49, 50, 58
Population, 51
Poverty, 54, 79–81, 92, 96, 130
Power, 76–84, 140
Practical People, 126
Producer, The 11, 106–7
Production & Investment, 14,
  46–9, 117
Productivity, 48
Profligacy, 6, 103

Recycling, 50
Resources, 49–51
Result, The 127–131

Scarcity, 13
Semi-Luxuries, 107–9
Shopping, 52–3, 91, 128
Smith, Adam 7, 61
Snag, The 131–4
Socialism, 9–10, 87
Staff, The 106
Supplier, The 105–6

Taxation, 108–9
Third World, 6, 16, 49 et seq., 54

Training, Education & 71–2, 120
  et seq,
Transport, 17–38
  Accident Casualties, 25,
    29–30, 151
  Alternative Scenario, 26 et seq,
  CAPITAL Assets, 18, 27
  Casualties, 25, 29–30, 151
  Congestion, 24, 37
  Convenience, 33
  Efficiency, 37
  Energy Consumption, 28–9,
    150
  Freight, 25, 27, 149
  Frequency, 32
  Future Technology, 38
  Manpower, 34–5, 152
  Nationalisation, 17–8
  Passengers, 26–7, 148
  Pollution, 30–1
  Public, 92
  Quality of Service, 32–3
  Railways, 17–20
  Roads, 20 et seq,
  Somerset & Dorset Railway, 18
  Speed, 31–2
  Summary, 35
  Underground, 19
  Volume of Goods, 34
  Work, To 22–3

Unemployment, 14, 89–90
Unions, 122
United Nations, 102, 133–4
Utopia, 5–6, 11, 60, 64, 96–8, 127,
  138

Valuing Ourselves, 57–9
Violence, 143

Waste, 10, 49, 88–100, 119, 139
Wealth, 9
Wooster, Bertie 67
Work, 48–9, 67 et seq,
  124–6, 138